D1557883

REFRAMING THE CONSTITUTION:

An Imperative for Modern America

By

LELAND D. BALDWIN

Santa Barbara, California

Oxford, England

1972

JK
31
B34

© 1972
By
LELAND D. BALDWIN

All rights reserved. This book or any part thereof may not be reproduced in any form without the written permission of the author.

342.73
B181

Library of Congress Catalog Card No. 78-187927
SBN Paperbound Edition 0-87436-082-X
Clothbound Edition 0-87436-083-8

Printed and bound in the United States of America

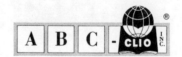

American Bibliographical Center—Clio Press

Riviera Campus, 2040 Alameda Padre Serra
Santa Barbara, California
Oxford, England

REFRAMING THE CONSTITUTION

ERRATA

Page

18   Quotation, line 6—"diminutive"

32   See CHICAGO, line 2—"w. of 89°"

53   See A GREATER OREGON, line 8—Williamette should read "Willamette"

110   Last line—delete "so"

121   See Section 8, line 5—change to read ". . . another without the consent of three-fourths of both the Congress and the Senate."

141   See (4)—change to read ". . . shall be abolished except in those cases . . ."

AMERICAN BIBLIOGRAPHICAL CENTER · CLIO PRESS
Riviera Campus, 2040 Alameda Padre Serra, Santa Barbara, California 93103

DEDICATED
TO
THAT GROUP OF MEN WHO MET IN PHILADELPHIA
IN THE SPRING AND SUMMER OF 1787
AND WROUGHT BETTER THAN THEY KNEW

MAY 4 - 1973

REFRAMING THE CONSTITUTION:
An Imperative for Modern America

TABLE OF CONTENTS

ACKNOWLEDGEMENTS

It is only fitting to note that I have referred to the literature of political science frequently in the preparation of this volume. In a personal sense I am indebted to those political scientists who were my colleagues in the University of Pittsburgh, notably Holbert N. Carroll, James C. Charlesworth, and the late Louis W. H. Johnston; also to Thomas Garden Barnes, English constitutional historian of the University of California at Berkeley; to Lloyd Garrison, political scientist turned editor; and to Edward McNall Burns, once of Rutgers, who is both political scientist and historian. Their vigorous and often valid objections were of great assistance in preparing the final draft, but they should not be blamed for any faults the reader may find with the result. Professor Johnston, with his inimitable realism, noted that since my essay was bound to excite thoughtless ridicule as much as thoughtful and constructive criticism, I should go ahead and say exactly what I wished to say. I have taken his advice, and consequently the text sometimes carries a note of self-assurance which I hope will stimulate rather than inhibit debate over a subject that is controversial in any context.

I am grateful to Donald Davidson and his staff of the library of the University of California at Santa Barbara for the free use of the library's facilities. Also I would like to acknowledge the aid of Dean James U. Rundle of Middlesex (Connecticut) Community College who, as so often in the past, has helped me through many an organizational and rhetorical thicket. Finally, I acknowledge the wise counsel of my wife, whose forbearance during my periods of intense study and patience in typing uncounted drafts made possible the completion of this work.

Leland D. Baldwin
Santa Barbara, California   Emeritus Professor of History
1972   University of Pittsburgh

INTRODUCTION

AUT CAESAR AUT NIHIL?

For years not a day has passed without some reference in print or video to the inadequacies and dangers of the American system of government and its practices. Though it has not always seemed to occur to those who wrote or spoke, analysis reveals that many of the problems they describe, whether domestic or foreign, have resulted in some degree from the faults and inadequacies of the Constitution. I do not intend to denigrate that document, for it fitted its "frame of reference" when it was written, and in many ways the authors wrought better than they knew. But that does not mean their work will fit the needs of representative democracy for all time.

It is evident that we have allowed dry rot to work at the very scaffolding on which we stood so boldly while manning the ramparts of freedom. I do not refer primarily to subversion, but to things far more subtle—rigid conservatism, sterile liberalism, and a new idealism uninformed by historical knowledge and not influenced by common sense. I refer also to environmental pollution, and even more significantly to overpopulation and the problems it brings. Solutions for these problems may demand not only that we give up some of our freedoms but that we alter some of the moral precepts on which our present culture is founded. We may eventually have to face the dilemma expressed in the motto of Cesare Borgia—Either Caesar or Nothing.

It would be naive to suppose that this dry rot is of recent origin, and I shall try to show that the fungi have been attacking the timbers of our cultural, Constitutional, and political system since its foundation. Certainly economic reforms become more difficult with each passing decade. There have been, on occasion, good and effective reforms, but all too often reforms have been nothing more than what Richard Hofstadter called "ceremonial solutions." The New Deal, though it should be credited with far greater accomplishments than the New Left will concede, did not always go to the root of our national problems. Perhaps it could not, for the people were not ready. Resistance to radical change seems to be characteristic of the English-speaking peoples. They traditionally demand that political and social innovations enter the cultural milieu in the guise of something old and familiar.

Enormous difficulties stand in the way of accomplishing the changes I shall propose. Ever since Washington assumed office as the first President, thoughtful men in each generation have worried about our Constitutional dilemmas, and have proposed a variety of remedies. During the last twenty years political scientists have written a great deal on the subject; unfortunately, their proposals have seldom gone to the heart of the problems but rather have merely suggested the need for such things as bigger and more expert staffs to serve the Congressional committees; changes in the seniority system; institution of question hours in the House and Senate; and a greater measure of party control of the membership and responsibility for legislation.

It may be that political scientists are so engrossed in theory and quantification that they have no time to study the decisive institutional changes that seem essential to me. One political scientist suggested that the changes proposed in this volume would make the President the master of Congress—another was convinced they would make the President the creature of Congress!

Institutions and the men who create them combine to make history. But as they age, institutions lose their force and often become irrelevant. Then the will of a strong man or a small group of men assumes unwonted significance. Very likely we would not have seen the rise of the Russian Soviets without the will of Lenin, or the Vietnam tragedy without the will of Lyndon Johnson. In Russia and the United States, national institutions became irrelevant to the needs of the time, or so close to irrelevant that the will of one man could rule or convince. Changes ordinarily come slowly, but when institutions lose their relevance to current conditions, revolutionary change may occur with startling and catastrophic rapidity.

I therefore propose changes relevant enough to promise a solution to our problems, but not radical enough to destroy our traditional democratic ideals. Our formerly homogeneous parties seem to be moving toward an ideological split, and that movement may ultimately prove to be destructive of democracy. In the face of such movements we must earnestly seek effective ways to preserve our common allegiance to democracy, and ways to preserve the formalized nature of the political struggle. If we cannot, the alternative may well be the "man on horseback."

I assume that Americans—like their British predecessors—will consent to some changes in substance so long as familiar names and symbols are retained. We need to find a way to introduce changes, some of them merely technical, that will encourage more effective and more flexible government. None of these proposals entail serious changes in our basic democratic ideology. I am thoroughly in accord with American political ideals—freedom and the rights of the individual—and wish to see them applied to the solution of such critical problems as environmental pollution, poverty, and racism before the problems engulf us. I propose no repeal of Supreme Court decisions, and on the whole wish to reaffirm our heritage of rights, duties, and privileges. The few changes that verge on the radical are chiefly at the one point where solutions to certain internal and international problems might be interpreted as beyond the scope of our present Constitution. We need to introduce institutional changes that can produce more flexible responses to our problems.

I am fully aware, of course, that solutions do not necessarily follow on technical changes. Human beings are strange creatures, given to voting their prejudices as much as their likes or even their selfish interests. They sometimes give way to a mass hysteria that no Constitution and no laws can restrain. They have been known at times to climb a restraining fence in order to jump into a snake pit.

A characteristic of the melting pot is that it melts very slowly—ethnic antipathies and rivalries have flourished for generations. Ethnic factors may have had as much to do with the success of the New Deal as economic hardship and the party loyalty of urban machines and Southern courthouse gangs. The new association of the Democratic Party with the liberal Establishment may presage a change in those loyalties. We may see a reversal of the traditional loyalties of the Southern courthouse gangs who may well become Republican and unite with the hard-hat sons of the Okies and production-line workers in mutual resentment of Negroes, Puerto Ricans, Cubans, Chicanos, and the privileged children of the middle class.

The present state of public opinion may make it difficult to alter the federal system and its division of powers between States and nation, the separation of powers between the Congress, the executive, and the judiciary, or the checks and balances. Yet it is clear that changes are necessary. Some elements of these principles need to be retained, but they must be made fruitful instead of merely obstructive. The proposals made here are not intended to be a dogmatic brief; they are intended to emphasize the need for a revision of the Constitution—and indeed it may be wiser and more practical proposals that will eventually bring about the desired results.

But the debate should begin.

I believe that many of our social and political problems arise from the defects in our Constitution or have been fostered by our constitutional system. These defects and the proposed remedies are discussed at some length in the text. They are merely enumerated here.

The essential thesis of this book is two-fold. First, the electorate does not have the expertise to propose the details of legislation or administration, or to serve as constant and informed guardians of the public welfare. Therefore some provision should be made in the Constitution for such guardians and at the same time for a greater degree of legislative and administrative flexibility. On the other hand, and second, neither legislators, administrators, nor guardians should be allowed to operate in disregard of the public will; therefore the electorate should have more effective power than it has at present to force the government to take notice of that will.

To come to specific ills and the proposed remedies:

(1) *The division of powers* between States and nation leads to obstruction and inefficiency. Furthermore, the States are no longer viable—they are antiquated, clumsy, antipathetic toward each other, and no longer capable of performing their functions.

I shall therefore propose that state sovereignty be modified—some critics will say abandoned—in favor of the creation of larger and more viable States, each formed so far as feasible upon community of problems. Their constitutions should be framed to provide for renovated legislative, executive, and judicial processes, and for more efficient local governments. Moreover, their powers should expand or contract as needful and as their representatives in Congress decide, but with due obeisance to the principle that all possible powers should be wielded by the States.

(2) *The separation of powers* between the three branches of government is so rigid that it obstructs progress and imperils national safety. The Executive and the Congress are at loggerheads because some of the checks and balances written into the Constitution are outdated. The President represents a national electorate but the legislative power is vested in a House of Representatives and a Senate whose jealous members represent purely local interests and are incapable of molding national policy. Consequently, Congress is dilatory and obstructive while the President is forced to assume emergency powers that often border on dictatorship. And the obsolete Electoral College must be displaced and a rational method found to elect the President.

Here I shall propose that the Congress become a unicameral body which includes a President, who is chosen along with the majority of the body, but with Constitutional provisions which make both more sensitive to changing public opinion. Separate from Congress I shall propose a reconstructed Senate, partly appointed from slates furnished by the States, which shall act as a court of last resort and a board of censors and ombudsmen, charged with guardianship of the public welfare and a limited oversight of legislation. Its presiding officer would be a Chief Justice who would also serve as titular Chief of State, thus relieving the President of part of his crushing duties.

(3) *The party system* must be renovated to make the separation of powers effective. At present, effective government requires the President's party to have a Congressional majority in favor of the President's program. This rarely happens. American national parties have always been amorphous alliances of local and State interests. Historically the system has been obstructive—frequently requiring labored policy and legislative compromises which do not and cannot solve problems. The system worked fairly well when there was time to spare but it is dangerous when events move swiftly and crisis follows crisis. The party system must be made more responsible for the solution of problems and more responsive to public opinion. The parties must be made to keep platforms and programs up to date and to provide effective leadership not only for the majority party but for the "loyal opposition." All this must be done while preserving reasonable checks against hasty or ill-considered legislation.

My proposals envision Constitutional provisions for the organization of parties, the selection of candidates, the holding of conventions, and the governing and financing of campaigns—all under the general supervision of the reconstructed Senate.

(4) *Rule by majority* is not considered in the Constitution (indeed most of the framers abhorred the thought). Yet majority rule arose, at least in part, from faults written into the document and its early amendments. John C. Calhoun formulated his doctrine of the "concurrent majority" (or "voice") during the 1820's in the hope that it would avoid a tyranny over the Southern minority by the Northern majority. Alexis de Tocqueville's analysis of American society and government written a few years later was a classic forecast of the effects of majority rule. De Tocqueville made it clear that his criticism of majority rule was based on the failure of the Constitutions (Federal and State) to limit the overwhelming power of the majority. He said:

> The authority of a king is purely physical, and it controls the actions of the subject, without subduing his private will; but the majority possesses a power which is physical and moral at the same time; it acts upon the will as well as upon the actions of men, and it represses not only all contest, but all controversy. I know no country in which there is so little true independence of mind and freedom of discussion as in America.[1]

Perhaps the current threat of polarization and civil war represents a greater danger to the American political system than a majoritarian tyranny. On the other hand, a study of history reveals that deep civil divisions may often presage the rise of a dictator. The United States has been fortunate throughout its brief history because potential revolutionaries—at least the whites—have been pacified by gifts of land. Dissidents in the early years escaped *some* of the social pressures

---

[1]See *Democracy in America* (2v., 1845), 1:285 for his exposition.

either by moving to thinly settled parts of the West or by moving to a different community. Moving from one community to another can still be a form of refuge and it is possible for the modern American to "lose" himself in a city. But, computers, credit bureaus, draft boards, police records, and the FBI make it impossible to escape entirely from the will of the effective majority. More and more people refuse to accept bureaucratic rules as an expression of the majority view and their dissent is too often violent.

The citizen in our computerized society often despairs of resolving the dilemma posed by impersonal centralization on one side and runaway democracy on the other. This dilemma can be met only by the most careful consideration by thoughtful men and women. As will be seen, I envision the Senate as composed of just such men and women, but the provision that its membership is continually refreshed by new appointees should ensure that it does not become so rarified that it loses sight of the public welfare or of the individual citizen.

The events of recent years make it clear that the above-named problems must be resolved, whether or not the specific remedies I propose are adopted. The country's leadership is often honestly divided, but it is also clear that all too often there is a spirit of bigotry and intolerance in the face of changing social conditions which may well result in the disintegration of the nation. More likely the situation will deteriorate until at last—God save us!—a leader will emerge who will do for the United States what Caesar did for Rome, Cromwell for England, and Napoleon for France.

Chapter 1

THE SOURCES OF AMERICAN DEMOCRACY

THE PURITAN ETHIC

The conjunction of the Puritan ethic and the abundance of natural resources is doubtless responsible for the American obsession with production and ever more production, with its attendant ills: waste and planned obsolescence, imperialism, pollution of the environment—even, perhaps, for the specter of nuclear holocaust that haunts us. But the inescapable fact is that without this American obsession the world could not have learned how to conquer scarcity and open the way to the era of abundance of which Utopians had always dreamed.

The American Puritan ethic arose out of the Reformation (chiefly from Calvinism) and was carried from England and Scotland to America. Puritan man had abandoned his comfortable niche in the medieval hierarchy and stood face to face with God, with no priest or galaxy of saints to intercede for him. God had consigned the human race to eternal damnation but, for reasons known only to Himself, had reserved a few for salvation. But though preoccupied with the after-life, the Puritan was actively concerned with the here-and-now, and he dedicated himself to earning the tangible rewards which demonstrated that he had been "elected" for salvation. The diligent, the frugal, and the thrifty man—and therefore often the rich—was chosen of God and thus was confirmed in a belief in his own righteousness. On the other hand, the poor man was poor not merely because he was lazy, irresponsible, or unlucky, but because he was doomed to damnation.

Calvinism was rich in rationalizations, for its adherents were continually faced by contradictions. Nevertheless, it is clear that the system was based on an attempt to deal with the economy of scarcity that had plagued the world from prehistoric times. Under all its theological trimmings and rationalizations, Calvinism was groping toward the view that only by amassing capital and investing it in production could men enjoy a more plentiful way of life. Modern history has been the evolution of that idea, and nowhere more clearly than in the United States.

The claim has been made that the Puritan ethic was confined to the Northern and Middle colonies and their westward extensions, and that it was not found in the South. The adherents of this claim go on to state that the succession of Federalist, Whig, and Republican Parties regarded themselves as morally motivated—as set apart by God as his chosen political instruments. Conversely, the Democratic-Republican Party, founded by Jefferson and Madison and known through most of American history as the Democratic Party, was the party of the outsiders—the South, the Catholic immigrants, the unsuccessful farmers, the discontented and defeated.

There is a kernel of truth in this analysis, but it scarcely holds together when the South and the agricultural regions are sweepingly portrayed as being Democrats who rejected the Puritan ethic. The facts were more complicated. We will soon refer to John Locke, whose reputed ideas about the holding of property reinforced certain aspects of the Puritan ethic, and it is notable that he was studied in the South as well as the North. But the pristine version of the Puritan ethic also had a place in the South.

Perry Miller concludes that the literature produced in Virginia and by the founders of the colony who remained in England "exhibits a set of principles for guiding not a mercantile investment but a medieval pilgrimage." In other words, the founders of Virginia had much the same aims and ideals as those of New England who felt that they were building "a City of God." Virginians were just as aware as New Englanders that the tribulations and disasters they suffered were brought on them by Satan and, like their Northern neighbors, they believed in divine guidance.[1]

It is thus a mistake to represent the Puritan ethic as confined to the North and its extensions, for not only was it brought from England to the South, but the Scotch-Irish Presbyterians, the Baptists, and some of the strait-laced German sects implanted it in the Piedmont just east of the Appalachians and then joined their English confreres in carrying it over the mountains. The shorthand of American history textbooks has laid stress on the fox-hunting squires of Virginia's and Carolina's tidewater instead of the bigoted religious sects of the Great Valley,

---

[1]Perry Miller, "The Religious Impulse in the Founding of Virginia," in *The William and Mary Quarterly* 5:492-522 (Oct. 1948) and 6:24-41 (Jan. 1949).

and on the canting parsons and Samuel Sewalls of New England's seaward fringe and not on the Boston waterfront, Harvard's commencement binges, and a rum-soaked, wenching interior.

The rather common view that Puritanism would have been élitist without the influence of Jefferson and Jackson is misleading. In fact, the medieval English Lollards were levelers, and the leveling element was strong in Cromwell's Puritan army. English democracy owes nothing to Jefferson, for Puritanism, like many other human ideas, had within it the potential for both aristocracy and democracy. Ralph Barton Perry made that point clear a generation ago.[2]

PROPERTY AND THE SOCIAL COMPACT

In *The Laws of Ecclesiastical Polity* the English divine Richard Hooker (1553–1600) sought to reconcile the medieval concept of hierarchy with the natural rights of man and the origin of government as a compact among the people. The idea of the social compact was not the invention of Hooker, of course, but was found among the ancient Greeks, probably even before Plato. Moreover, it was a concept that could emerge spontaneously wherever a group of people were gathered beyond the pale of established government. Thus, whether they drew the idea from Hooker or the ancients, the Pilgrim Fathers signed the Mayflower Compact (1620) and the seceders from Massachusetts set up the Fundamental Orders of Connecticut (1639). The concept was to be extended in the writings of Locke and Rousseau and was to find nearly complete acceptance in the Convention of 1787, despite the dispute as to whether the Constitution was a compact among the States or among the people of the States.

The most complete early statement in England of the compact theory is found in the *Treatises on Government* (1690), by John Locke (1632–1704). Not only did Locke adopt the compact theory, but he went on to portray property as the rock on which social order was founded. Locke drew much of his inspiration from Hooker and thus his ideas—characteristic of Englishmen—were evolutionary rather than revolutionary. But when Locke was read in France, the milieu was so autocratic that his acceptance could be nothing less than revolutionary. This was soon demonstrated by the *Social Contract* (1762) of Jean Jacques Rousseau (1712–78), to which can be attributed much of the impetus for the French Revolution.

Some writers have attributed the American Revolution to Locke, and in a sense this is true, but in another sense the American Revolution was not a revolution but a confirmation of an existing condition.

---

[2]Perry's *Puritanism and Democracy* (New York: Vanguard, 1944) is the classic exposition of the interconnection of Puritanism and democracy.

There have been attempts to show that Locke's presentation of the role of property has been misrepresented or at least over-emphasized. Nevertheless, the belief that he upheld its soundness was eagerly accepted in both North and South. The difference was that Northern property took the form of ships, factories, and farms, while Southern capital consisted to a large extent of plantations and slaves, and these were the socially acceptable forms of wealth. Nevertheless, there was a Southern class of businessmen—bankers, factors, lawyers, land speculators, and storekeepers—and they tended to join with the planters in the Whig Party.

Jefferson's Declaration of Independence adopted Locke's doctrine of natural rights and in its original form stated these as the right to "life, liberty, and property." It is said that Franklin objected to the holding of property as a natural right, and so "the pursuit of happiness" was substituted. Nevertheless, Locke's concept of the holding and protection of property as the balance wheel of society was accepted and has become a fundamental of American democratic ideology.

THE COLONIAL DEMOCRATIC STRUGGLE

Democratic evolution was inherent in English institutions, and Englishmen brought the consciousness of this fact to these shores. True, in England the right to share in government was in the period of settlement regarded as pretty well confined to those who held a "stake in society"—that is, the property holders. In America most of the settlers sooner or later became land holders, and as such they demanded a share in government. The demand was voiced in each colony and led to a struggle between those with considerable property and social standing and those with less of each. The result was numerous tumults and a number of open rebellions, most of which are not even mentioned in college texts. Of course, the causes of these disturbances were often more complex than a mere struggle between big and little property, but it was there that the nub of the controversy lay—and has lain to our own day.

One can see in this struggle one aspect of the fulfillment of Calvinism and its more or less unconscious search for plenty. The abundance of land had given to the many the stake in society (land) that carried with it the right to share in government. Land was one form of the capital upon which Calvinism laid much stress, and this helps explain why Americans were so far ahead of Europe in evolving democratic institutions. Democracy posits equality, and this equality is evidenced either by land, goods, or (today) by the right to a job.

Beyond the internal struggles there lay a struggle between the colonies and the Crown—eventually between the colonies and Parliament as the latter took over the functions of the Crown. By 1775 there had evolved two concepts of the structure of the Empire. The British regarded it as an aggregation of states (the United Kingdom, Ireland, and the colonies) governed by a Parliament elected by the people of Great Britain. The King was still regarded as the Executive, but the

Cabinet was in process of taking over his powers, though this fact was not as yet universally recognized.

Americans regarded the Empire as a congeries of states—what we would call a federation—each of them self-governing but recognizing a common head, courteously known as the sovereign. Parliament could legislate for the King in matters that were indubitably of common imperial interest and after due consultation with the colonies, but it could not interfere in the internal affairs of any state other than the United Kingdom. Thus it could not levy taxes on the colonies, save for the minimal customs duties necessary to regulate trade with the world outside the Empire.

Americans pointed out that English laws and customs were based on government by elected representatives, and that they were not represented in Parliament. British legalists retorted that representation was not a function of geography— that, indeed, some of the most populous cities in the kingdom had no members in Parliament. According to this theory Americans were *virtually represented* by the members of Parliament elected in Great Britain. On that point the two sides were at an impasse, for Americans were represented in their colonial assemblies by men elected from strictly defined geographical districts.

The long struggle for self-rule within the colonies and between the colonies and the Crown had confirmed the view that democracy is an evolutionary process and not merely a function of the structure of government. This was expressed in several conditions backed by firm beliefs:

1. The franchise was relatively widespread among property holders and those with certain standards of income.

2. Special legal class privileges had practically disappeared, and there was a virtual equality before the law.

3. The people were still actively seeking to widen their political and economic rights; especially were they concerned with widening the franchise and thus gaining a greater control over public policy.

4. They were deeply concerned with confirming their rights within the Empire, and in this effort there was essential unity between the opponents in the internal struggle.

It can readily be seen that the above conditions and beliefs were based on the acceptance of the compact theory. Not only that, but there was a growing conviction that the terms of the compact should be set down in writing, as they actually were in the charters held by several of the New England colonies and by Pennsylvania and Delaware. While the concept of evolutionary democracy came from England, by 1775 the Thirteen Colonies had passed the mother country in the application. Not only did they understand that democracy was process (not structure) but they grasped the necessities of civil liberties; of popular control of the legislature and of its check on executive and judiciary; of the danger inherent in the union of church and state; and, finally, that concentration of economic power in a few hands leads to abuses and eventual loss of liberty. Perhaps it would be wrong to say that they had worked out in detail their definition of democracy and set up its tests, but they were moving toward them purposefully and intelligently.

The simplest definition of democracy in practice is "rule by the people," as Abraham Lincoln put it, "government of the people, by the people, for the people." Democracy is not a perfect form of government but it emphasizes flexibility—the willingness to attend to new ideas and to use them. There are three standards by which democratic government can be judged:

1. The extent to which the people are governed by law, and not by the capricious whims of the rulers. In a democracy the citizen has recourse to the courts, and the duty of the courts is to judge whether the law in question is in accord with the fundamental principles on which the laws are based.

2. The extent to which progressive compromises are effected while the basic integrity of civil liberties is maintained.

3. The extent to which democracy is viewed as a continuing process rather than a rigid structure of government.

Democratic government can never lay claim to perfection, and so the test of democracy does not depend on the form and structure of either the Constitution or the institutions of government. Rather, it should be tested against a standard of flexibility and the degree to which it is open-ended—whether the people can replace their executive and their legislators with others more to their liking. There are, inevitably, shortcomings in the practice of democracy—only a part of the people may share in government at any given moment—but if the government is open-ended and if its institutions leave the way open for change, it meets the basic test of democracy.

ORDER AND LIBERTY

Inherent in the above description of democracy is the fact that it can be maintained only if a tension is established and maintained among competing interests in both society and government. As we shall see, this was one of the most difficult problems that confronted the Framers of the Constitution of 1787. In order to explain the problem more clearly, let us pass beyond the colonial and Revolutionary periods to the famous struggle between Hamilton and Jefferson.

There has been a rather general tendency to represent Hamilton as championing a strong central government, the dominance of commerce and manufactures, and rule by the rich and the well-born. Against him is placed Jefferson, standing for a weak central government, the dominance of agriculture, and rule by the people as a whole. This is, at best, a superficial view. During the first twenty years of the republic we find either the two leaders or their followers deliberately contradicting in word or deed every item of their trilogy of tenets, and there is a lesson in that fact. No one can be quite so pure and moral about "principles" as a party out of power; no one sees so readily as a group of men in power that facts must be dealt with on their own terms. Nevertheless, the original cast of mind remains, and each will deal with a situation as nearly as possible in conformity with its basic beliefs and hopes.

The basic principles of Hamilton and Jefferson—as distinguished from the above tenets—lie much deeper. They can perhaps be best expressed in the two concepts "order" and "liberty." Hamilton claimed, quite rightly, that without order progress is impossible, for men would not be safe in their lives or their property. Jefferson's answer was that rigid order could easily become the bulwark erected by the wealthy to protect their status and property, while they used their power to destroy liberty and oppress their fellow citizens; as he saw it, the people's control of government was their chief protection against predatory capitalism. Hamilton could well have replied that the individualism implied by complete liberty inevitably meant that those favored by luck, initiative, or shrewdness would amass wealth and with it the power to oppress their fellows.

Hamilton did not reject liberty, of course; he simply believed that it must give precedence to good order, in the sense of stability. Jefferson did not reject order; he simply believed that order without liberty is of no value.

Both believed that where a man's treasure is, there will his heart be also. Hamilton looked on order and property as treasures that are responsibly guarded only if they are entrusted to the select few. Property, as the foundation of good order, must be preserved from direct injury or from limitations that prevent it from multiplying itself freely. Obviously, the Jeffersonians did not reject the holding of property or its role as the foundation of good order; they simply believed that property should be widely disseminated and should not become an instrument that could be used for limiting the rights, snatching the livelihood, or besmirching the dignity of the individual.

When Jefferson retired from the Presidency to Monticello, he placed Hamilton's bust opposite his own in the great hall of the mansion, and there they still stand as symbols of the two great forces of democratic evolution. Hamilton may not have thoroughly understood the necessity of preserving the tension between order and liberty, but Jefferson did. Jefferson never held that democracy could acquire a final, static form when either order or liberty could be automatically assured—hence his recommendation of "a little rebellion now and then." Thinking in eighteenth-century terms, he believed that tension could best be preserved by strengthening free farmers as counters to the "aristocracy" of wealth—he meant plutocracy—who, like spiders at the center of a web, sat in the cities and manipulated the "real" producers of wealth, the farmers and planters.

Born on the Virginia frontier and familiar with its ideal of equality, Jefferson yet recognized that equality may promote mediocrity and thus hamper the initiative essential to progress. He recognized that the pioneers—and, for that matter, Americans in general—were far from being complete individualists but were subjected to intense social pressure. As he put it, "the inquisition of public opinion overwhelms in practice the freedom asserted by the laws in theory." But to the "aristocratic" claim that the people were not fit to govern themselves Jefferson answered in his First Inaugural Address: "Have we found angels in the form of men to govern them?" Then, after twenty-five more years filled with disappointments and frustrations he added with unquenchable faith: "I know of no safe depository of the ultimate powers of society but the people themselves; and if we think them not enlightened enough to exercise their control with a wholesome discretion, the remedy is not to take it from them, but to inform their discretion by education."

These two basic democratic phenomena—tension and education—have so permeated American thinking that, despite numerous aberrations, it is quite proper to speak of the United States as Jeffersonian in its ideology.[3]

THE PATRIARCHAL SOUTH

During the nineteenth century, political and economic ideas were so assiduously carried back and forth between the parties by splinter groups that the historian despairs of drawing hard and fast lines between the two political currents that have so often been represented as antithetical. All he can do is draw generalizations, and only then with caution.

Thus with all due caution we may suggest that the South did not differ from the North because it rejected the Puritan ethic or had no capacity to industrialize —indeed, the angry God of Massachusetts had been expelled by Unitarianism and taken refuge in the South, bringing with him Puritan fundamentalism and renewing the region's allegiance to medieval hierarchy. The difference lay rather in that the South unfortunately was held in the grip of the institution of slavery. This meant that it stubbornly insisted that human beings could be regarded as property, and that the slave owner held over his slaves the same capitalistic rights that the Northern factory owner held over big property. The South saw itself as struggling against unreasonable odds to preserve property rights. It feared change lest change bring freedom to the slaves and let loose on society a numerous class that was regarded as lacking in moral sense and the ability to exercise the Puritan and Lockean virtues of thrift and self-reliance. This view of human beings as property was a significant factor in hewing out the Constitution, and was to play a significant role until the Civil War. But the Puritan virtues existed alongside slavery, and it is well to point out that a strong wing of the Whig Party was manned by the planters and businessmen of the South; it was only the crisis of secession that drove them into the Democratic Party. Moreover, Manifest Destiny found its chief support in the South and in New York City's cotton factors.

Under the circumstances it seems fair to attribute to slavery much of the

---

[3]The above treatment of Hamilton and Jefferson is adapted from my *Stream of American History,* Fourth Edition (New York: Van Nostrand Reinhold Co., 1969), pages 158-159.

responsibility for the survival in the South of the medieval view of society as a static corporation, a hierarchy with a father-king at the head. The British form of this belief, best set forth in Sir Robert Filmer's *Patriarcha, or the Natural Power of Kings* (1680), had been brought to the Thirteen Colonies, where it was transmuted into the patriarchal family. In his *Treatises on Government* Locke attacked Filmer's father-king concept by setting up against it his adaptation of Richard Hooker's natural rights of man, which was to become the guidon of the American revolutionists.

The long struggle to protect human rights from encroachment by property rights has dominated so much of American history it has obscured the fact that the patriarchal ideal survived and flourished in the South, and even in some rural areas of the North. The patriarchal farm family became the basic social and economic institution of the South, with the father as the dominant figure and the other members falling into their proper positions in the group. Such an institution depended on two things: the possession of land and the purity of the blood line —hence the antebellum Southerner's fierce protection of the chastity of his women, while at the same time he was willing to scatter his seed among women of lower status, especially slave women, because the progeny took the status of the mothers.

The patriarchal South was, and to some extent still is, a closed hierarchical society. One can belong if he can establish an identity—that is, prove the legitimacy of his blood relationship to an established family. This helps explain the care with which families in the Deep South, however down on their luck they may be, trace their faintest connections with the First Families of Virginia or the Cavalier settlers of South Carolina; it confirms their position in the hierarchy of blood and status. Inevitably there is a certain romantic inflation of facts, which W. J. Cash expressed as the ability of a Southerner to boast in one breath of his descent from the Red Kings of Ireland and in the next of being a self-made man.

Anyone who is familiar with the South even today, or who reads William Faulkner's novels, must be impressed by the significance attributed to ties to the land—preferably a certain piece of land—and to purity of the blood line. "Black blood" or "Indian blood" contaminates the progeny of the most aristocratic father—but the connection does not contaminate the father himself. Nevertheless, the patriarchal view of society potentially makes a place in the hierarchy for everyone, and even "nigras" have their assigned status and the right to a share of loyalty and protection. But the patriarchal view also insists on hierarchy, and Southern opposition to desegregation is doubtless based in some part on the fear that it will end in a "debasement" of the blood line and the end of the patriarchal hierarchy.[4]

---

[4]This cursory view of the patriarchal South is expanded in readable form in Keith McKean's brief *Cross Currents in the South* (Denver: Alan Swallow, 1960). More extensive is Wilbur J. Cash, *The Mind of the South* (N.Y.: Knopf, 1941), which goes into the effects of the frontier on the Southern patriarchal idea; it has been accused of giving the "hillbilly" view of the South but, after all, the Appalachian highlanders did people much of the South.

The survival of the hierarchic ideal in the South is significant because it can become the core of an authoritarian offensive, as it has already in several notable instances. If a Caesar ever rises in the United States, he will not resemble the great Julius, or Oliver Cromwell, or Napoleon Bonaparte. He will be a peculiarly American product, doubtless coming into power under the cloak of populism. We have already seen this authoritarian figure foreshadowed in Huey Long and George Wallace.

THE PURITAN ETHIC AND THE NEED FOR CHANGE

It is now clear that the Puritan ethic has been greatly weakened, and probably is passing away. In other words, the economy of scarcity is being replaced by an economy of abundance. In a very real sense this is a proof of the success of the Puritan ethic. Moreover, it is questionable if democracy could continue to exist indefinitely in a world governed by scarcity. This does not by any means imply that abundance will cover the world—or that, even if it does, democracy will flourish. Indeed, as stated in the introduction, we face an array of problems that must be solved or mankind may be pushed back to an age of simple agriculture or be forced to accept either authoritarianism or totalitarianism. We shall take up some of these problems later on. At the moment my purpose is to trace very briefly the steps that have led to the economy of abundance in the United States.

In the first place, it is well to qualify the American belief that historically we have been almost complete individualists. I question very much the rather common belief that antebellum Americans, in either North or South, were "inner directed." True, there did exist a certain individualism which found its greatest scope on the frontier—that is, at the very edge of advancing settlement. But behind the frontier, in the thinly settled agricultural West, social pressures tended to hold individualism in check.

Of course the pressures differed in the Old Northwest and the Old Southwest. The greater strength of the Puritan ethic in the North probably accounts for the fact that nearly every community there had a common school and nearly every county an academy. In contrast, the concept of hierarchy probably accounts for the relative scarcity of common schools in the South and the relative abundance of colleges attended by the sons of the gentry. Probably there was a broader scope for individualism in the Old Southwest; for one thing, greater sexual license was possible because of the presence of slave women. Religion exercised certain restraints, but there was a considerable amount of antinomianism—if one professed the faith, he was saved from hell and could then let himself go with liquor, cards, women, thievery, and violence. It is difficult to be sure at this late date, but it may be that the antinomianism of the North was hypocritical while that of the South was honest, however naive it may have been.

At any rate it is inaccurate to speak of the North as more "revivalistic" than the South. Emotional revivalism was quite likely more rampant in the South, where it was busily laying the foundations of what H. L. Mencken was later to call the Bible Belt. But there was a distinct difference in the religion of the two regions. In the South, religion became the principal support of the status quo and presently gave sanction to the doctrine that slavery, far from being an evil, was a positive good. The revivalism of the North tore down the Calvinists' rationalized indifference to poverty and began the great benevolent and reform movement of the 1830's, including a crusade against slavery. But, in the Calvinist tradition, religion in the North also encouraged—even stimulated—the brand of individualism that devoted itself to amassing wealth.

Since this is not a political history of the United States, it is not necessary to follow in detail the evolution of political parties. The early Constitutional struggle between agriculture on one side and trade, industry, and finance on the other was soon complicated by the passing of elements in each to the opposing party. The slavery question divided agriculture and forced Southern businessmen into the Democratic Party, while Northern businessmen and free farmers formed an uneasy alliance devoted to saving the Union. The Civil War perpetuated the division, and its influence on political and economic thought is still evident more than a century later. Nor should one forget the part played throughout by the presence of Negroes, not merely as a separate race but first as slaves and later as something analogous to peons—or even serfs. This is a favorite horrible example offered by New Left critics of the Establishment's ability to accept a reform but empty it of all meaning.

The criticism seems to hold water. No doubt many blacks were unprepared for the responsibilities of citizenship and economic independence, but regarded freedom as the right to lead an idle life and be fed by the government. On the other hand, thousands of the freedmen were skilled craftsmen and even professionals, and hundreds of thousands were eager to work and to learn. The disgraceful fact is that neither North nor South made a serious effort to give land to the freedmen and to educate them to assume their new responsibilities.

This was a sad mistake, especially since it takes time to instill the Puritan ethic of thrift and hard work. In fact, at that very time industrialists were complaining of the way *white* laborers would work only long enough to buy a little food and whiskey and then lay off work for several weeks. Even in the South the typical poor white could neither read nor write, was quite indifferent to the economic side of the Puritan ethic, and took an interest in politics, when he did, largely for reasons that were racist or purely parochial. The Jeffersonian insistence that the democratic process could work only if the citizens were educated has seldom been more openly ignored.

Organized labor entered the political picture in the 1830's and, with the evolution of mass production and its promise of plenty, became more violently insistent on its right to share in American abundance. In the 1930's Franklin Roosevelt put together a coalition of farmers, laborers, blacks, intellectuals, and city machines that wrought tremendous changes in the social, political, and economic patterns of American life—changes which the younger generation all too often ignore or denigrate.

The 1960's saw the Roosevelt coalition begin to break up, but it is not yet clear what will take its place. Some Americans hope to end the traditional fuzzing of "principles" between the parties and substitute two straight ideological parties— conservative and liberal, or perhaps radical right and radical left. In the view of many observers, the demand for "instant Utopia" on the part of those who have not read history carefully, when joined to the growing penchant for violence, may result in the very polarization that the ideologists desire and sensible men dread. The result, unfortunately, is less likely to be a broadening of individualism and democracy than the ascendance, at least for a while, of the radical right.

At any rate, the old economy of scarcity seems to be passing and a new economy of abundance probably is dawning. Certain aspects of the Puritan ethic —thrift, hard work, venture capitalism—are rapidly being outdated as machines take the place of men. Our traditional form of democracy abhors sudden, disruptive change; that is why neither Progressivism, the New Deal, nor the Great Society ever completed its work. But equally evident is the fact that the transition now in progress has demonstrated that the old leisurely political ways made possible by our "infinite resources" are no longer feasible, and that a Constitution drawn up to ensure the slow pace of change is now outdated.

Chapter 2

PHILADELPHIA IN RETROSPECT

THE CONSTITUTIONAL CONVENTION: ACHIEVEMENT OR FAILURE?

The Constitution, now approaching its second centennial, has been in effect longer than any other written constitution. Despite the effects of custom, precedent, legislative interpretation, judicial review, executive action, and amendment, the wording of the document remains very much like the instrument signed by the thirty-nine Founding Fathers on September 17, 1787. There have been only four truly fundamental changes:

1. The Federal government has become more democratized.
2. Slavery has been abolished.
3. Federal sovereignty has been given precedence over State sovereignty.
4. The guarantees of the Bill of Rights have been gradually imposed on the States through the Supreme Court's interpretation of the Fourteenth Amendment.

The detailed changes that have been made are not startling when viewed in the context of political and social events. It is significant that most of the recent amendments were adopted only after years of debate and delay. As stated before, there is an inborn resistance to radical change amongst the English-speaking peoples—at least it is clear that Americans demand that all new things enter the political system in the guise of something old and familiar.

The Constitution of 1787 was not a pristine instrument newly struck off by the hand of man. On the contrary, it consists largely of judicious adaptations of ancient, British, and colonial precedents. From England, the mother country, it accepted what Bolingbroke and Blackstone mistakenly represented as a *separation* of powers in the British government, a concept that had already found expression in the several State constitutions. It also copied the British bicameral legislature, and the vague wording of Article II permitted the President eventually to assume almost monarchical powers. It sought to balance social forces after the fashion which the French philosophers so admired in the British Constitution. The Constitution also reflected the compact theory attributed to Locke and Rousseau.

The Convention solved two problems that had plagued mankind for centuries. The conflict between national and local interests was resolved, at least temporarily, by dividing sovereignty between the nation and the States. The conflict between the metropolis and its dependencies was resolved by providing that new States be admitted on an equal footing with the old. These solutions were foreshadowed within the British Empire. As previously stated, Americans had argued that the Empire was, in reality, a federation and that its provincial assemblies were sovereign in the management of local affairs, while matters of common interest were managed by the King-in-Parliament after consultation with the colonies. The idea of the admission of dependent areas to equal status within a metropolis had been long since formalized in New England, where new towns were created and admitted to equal representation with the old. Assemblies in the Southern states had also created new counties and, albeit grudgingly, given them legislative representation.

A careful examination of the Constitution of 1787 in the light of contemporary prejudices, fears, expectations, and hopes raises the question of whether it was intended to implement effective government or block it. It was inevitable that this kind of question would be raised, because colonial Americans were concerned, above all else, with preserving the rights of the individual against the interference of a central government. Even advocates of strong government like Hamilton did not relish the thought of government interference. The Framers had barely emerged from their struggle against what they considered to be (perhaps paranoiacally) a tyrant, and the States were still torn by rival interests. Understandably, the Founding Fathers were thus fearful of a "monarchy" on one hand and the "mob" on the other—they were afraid of either too much executive power or too much democracy. Most of the Framers had no sympathy with democracy, which they equated more with license than with liberty. As a consequence, they sought to remove the common people as far as possible from a direct influence on government, though they were aware they could not go too far in that direction lest the Constitution be rejected by the people.

The Founding Fathers were probably more interested in establishing an effective national administration than they were in passing legislation. It seems clear that the President, for a generation, was considered to be no more than an administrator of Congressional acts. The concept of executive initiative as a function of government was abhorrent to the Framers. In essence they regarded King George's attempt to exercise what he called his "prerogative" in centralizing control of the British Empire as usurpation, an outright violation of law. The Founding Fathers, influenced as they were by the Enlightenment, believed in rational discussion and carefully agreed-upon solutions to political problems, and so they hedged against executive usurpation by dividing the powers of government.

The Framers cannot be blamed for not anticipating the complexities of the twentieth century. They lived in a relatively simple society, isolated from the quarrels of Europe, Asia, and Africa. They could hardly be expected to foresee the power accrued by private enterprise, individual entrepreneurs, and corporations—a power as menacing to liberty as the "monarchy" or the "mob."[1] Nor could they be expected to anticipate the invention of rapid communications and transportation which, in this century, have bred sudden crises and forced the President to assume more initiative than they envisioned. The several States, Congress, and the Supreme Court lack the means of providing viable alternatives to executive actions; therefore they cannot legitimately call the President's assumption of power a "usurpation."

Despite the fears and failures of the Framers, and especially now that we know more about the theory and practice of democratic government, it is evident that they wrought better than they knew. The events of this century poignantly prove how right they were to fear the sort of democracy that they defined as license, for it has sometimes resulted in anarchy. The liberals among the Framers were equally correct in noting that a government given power sufficient to maintain order constantly teeters on the edge of tyranny.

THE STRENGTHS OF AMERICAN CONSTITUTIONAL DEMOCRACY

The greatest strength, as well as the gravest weakness, in the American form of government was pungently underscored by Richard Neustadt when he remarked that the Constitution did not set up institutions wielding separate powers but separated institutions sharing powers. The document met the democratic test of being open-ended, but it did not set up direct rule by the people. This very fact made some of the Framers hope it would be stillborn. Nevertheless, the long

---

[1]However, Madison in Number 10 of *The Federalist* did foresee the rise of "factions . . . united and actuated by some common impulse of passion, or of interest, adverse to the rights of other citizens, or to the permanent and aggregate interests of the community." Though he may have referred primarily to political parties, yet he also indicated that some factions would be formed along economic lines.

struggle for self-rule within the colonies and between the colonies and the Crown had left the Framers with the certain knowledge that democracy is an evolution-ary process and not merely a function of the structure of government, and that it can be maintained only by tension among forces in society and government.

The first of these they met by providing for amendment, though the method has proved to be incredibly clumsy. The second they met by elaborate separation and division of powers, and by checks and balances. The system worked—for a while—only because there was plenty of time and it served a simply organized society. Indeed, since most men held that the "least government is the best government," the Constitution was quite generally regarded as a work of genius. And so it was, in the context of its times—but that does not mean that it should remain unchanged in every technical aspect.

Americans generally have failed to recognize that the essence of democracy is not simply "rule by the people" but rather hospitality to change and, hopefully, betterment. Consequently, millions of American voters are cynical about democracy because they have expected too much from it. The sheer populousness of the modern state and the complexity of its problems seem to reduce an election to nothing more than a plebiscite on whether to "throw the rascals out." That is, the election is chiefly the means by which the voting public registers its approval or disapproval of the trends the government has followed. Yet, despite their cynicism, most voters are willing, if we are to believe the opinion polls and statistical studies which appear in the press, to accept the judgments of their elected representatives. And most of them are sophisticated enough to realize that complex problems of government cannot be decided by a head count or by an elusive majority. Indeed, an amazing number of citizens neither have political opinions nor vote. These facts do not prove that America is not a democracy; rather they may imply that millions of Americans have the good sense not to make judgments on matters about which they know little or nothing.

The Framers of the Constitution deliberately created a system of checks and balances to create and preserve tensions between the nation and the States, between the branches of government, and among social and economic interests because they recognized that tensions are essential to the preservation—and the evolution—of democracy. As was previously pointed out, Hamilton and Jefferson dramatized a basic division which sorely afflicted the Framers. The Constitutional Fathers deliberately preserved the tension between order and liberty by recogniz-ing there must be change, but we may presume that they had in mind change at the ballot box, not by mobs in the streets or on the campus. American reform movements have never been root-and-branch crusades; they have been processes of pruning and fertilizing the old Tree of Liberty and grafting new branches onto it.

Another strength of American democracy has been the basic allegiance given by political parties and interest groups to the principles of our democratic process.

The parties have seldom been ideological entities; each of them has included members representative of many parts of the political spectrum. The major parties have avoided ideological stands—aside from a general agreement on democracy—and have conducted political battles in accordance with certain formalized rules, including a tacit agreement not to persecute each other. There are some indications, in this era, that agreement on the rules is in danger and that not since the Civil War have so many partisans seriously contemplated a resort to violence.

WEAKNESSES IN AMERICAN CONSTITUTIONAL DEMOCRACY

The weaknesses of the American constitutional system of democracy stem, paradoxically, from some of the same provisions that produce its greatest strengths. Take for example the condition just stated above: that democracy cannot function unless all the important elements of the society abide by the rules. Lincoln faced this danger in 1861. When he suspended the writ of habeas corpus in the case of John Merryman, he ignored the opinion of the Supreme Court and responded to the criticism of a group of protesters by saying: "Must I shoot a simple-minded soldier boy who deserts, while I must not touch a hair of a wily agitator who induces him to desert?" Lincoln thus met the eternal democratic dilemma between order and liberty by asserting that he would not permit the Constitution to stand in the way of preserving the democracy it had been established to protect.

Indeed, Americans have been a little too smug about having experienced only one serious revolution in almost two centuries. The fact is that the abundant resources of this continent have enabled the government to buy off the discontented, at first with land and now with welfare payments and subsidies. It may be suggested that this, even more than the virtues inherent in the Constitution, has ensured peace and more or less orderly progress. The role that America's natural resources have played in the formation and preservation of democracy— that of an effective obstacle to revolution—was readily grasped by Alexis de Tocqueville, who wrote:

> When the people rule, it must be rendered happy or it will overturn the state; and misery is apt to stimulate it to those excesses to which ambition rouses kings. The physical causes, independent of the laws, which contribute to promote general prosperity, are more numerous in America than they have ever been in any other country in the world, at any other period of history. In the United States, not only is legislation democratic, but nature herself favors the cause of the people.[2]

---

[2] *Democracy in America,* 1:318.

It is also possible that the tensions built into the Constitution would have obstructed effective government had it not been for the economic opportunities opened up by abundant land—and, of course, by the fact that post-colonial society was relatively simple in its organization and economy. During the first half-century, individuals in the United States could pretty much manage their own affairs without recourse to a central government. De Tocqueville also recognized this, and speculated that with growing complexity the central government would be forced to interfere more and more.

During the decades from about 1820 until 1860 the social, economic, technological, and moral problems facing the nation, especially in the North, became so complex that they were not readily resolvable by the political processes established in the Constitution. The result was civil war, and if President Lincoln had adhered strictly to the letter of the Constitution, the Union might have been permanently dissolved. One of the factors that added to the growing complexity of American society was the multiplicity of voluntary, non-political organizations which developed and proliferated during the nineteenth century. De Tocqueville commented:

> The political associations which exist in the United States are only a single feature in the midst of the immense assemblage of associations in that country. Americans of all ages, all conditions, and all dispositions, constantly form associations. They have not only commercial and manufacturing companies, in which all take part, but associations of a thousand other kinds—religious, moral, serious, futile, extensive or restricted, enormous or dimunitive. . . . Wherever at the head of some new undertaking you see the government in France, or a man of rank in England, in the United States you will be sure to find an association.[3]

These associations eventually grew into social, economic, and cultural federations that crossed party lines and supplemented the political federation established by the Constitution. (Current examples are the National Association for the Advancement of Colored People, the Save-the-Redwoods League, and John Gardner's Common Cause.) It may be that such voluntary federations cooled some of the heat of political combat and made it possible for the nation to remain fairly stable until the 1930's, except, of course, for the period of the Civil War. However, the complexities of the present era make the problems of the 1850's seem simple. We can no longer rely on the cushion of time or the luxury of "infinite" resources characteristic of policy making in the nineteenth century. Many of the Constitutional forms we have inherited are inadequate for the solution of modern problems.

---

[3] *Democracy in America*, 2:114.

CONSTITUTIONAL OBSTACLES TO DEMOCRATIC GOVERNMENT

The Constitution itself imposes certain obstacles to the rational solution of contemporary problems. First, it divides sovereignty between the nation and the States and thus marks out an arena for perpetual conflict. The compromise was necessary to obtain ratification by the States, but there can be no quasi-sovereignty, any more than there can be a quasi-virgin. The Civil War apparently settled the matter in favor of national sovereignty and the Union, but State sovereignty remains the shibboleth of rigid conservatives and reactionaries who oppose national in favor of parochial State interests.

The tragedy involved in this division of sovereignty has become clearer in our own day, when most States have lost their economic viability—if they ever had it. They are incapable of controlling the activities of corporations which possess financial power and managerial expertise greater than that available to State governments. The States are therefore subjected to pressures they are quite unable to resist. Their legislatures pass bills to favor special interests, and their Congressmen sometimes seriously hamper the effectiveness of the national government by representing unreasonable local demands in the Senate and House. The myth of State sovereignty and the continued representation of divergent local interests in the Congress hamper the ability of the national government to pass rational legislation. The faults of the federal system are evidenced by the long failure of Congress to pass effective civil rights legislation dealing with the black minority, and by the passage of clearly unconstitutional bills, such as the McCarran Internal Security Act (1950).

Second, the separation of powers among the legislative, executive, and judicial branches of government and the innumerable checks and balances exercised between them ensure that the government will be dilatory, cumbersome, and ineffective. Each branch of government is constitutionally ordained to obstruct the action of all the others. Each branch, under certain conditions, acquires and exercises powers that belong primarily to the others. The Supreme Court assumes the legislative power whenever it opines that the Congress or the States have been negligent in such matters as civil rights, equality of representation, or the racial integration of educational systems. The President, being the only official elected by a national constituency (although in the technical sense, not directly) has tended to visualize problems in a national or international context and to behave as though only the executive can act in the general interest. Accordingly, the President has assumed the power to make executive agreements with other nations and international bodies—even the power to commit the nation to war without the consent of Congress. Congress has sought, sometimes effectively and sometimes ineffectively, to curtail the assumed powers of the executive branch, and it is certainly arguable that the Congress, at least the Senate, has sometimes been wiser than the President.

Third, the shortcomings imposed by the federal division of powers and the system of checks and balances increase the level of conflict between the President and the Congress and between the Senate and House. Each branch is jealous of its own prerogatives, sometimes to the extent that each will act to block the passage of legislation needed to promote the national interest. Events since World War II demonstrate that the Congress, as it is now constituted, is often unable or unwilling to act with dispatch in the face of national or international emergencies. Similarly, the Congress cannot make up its mind in meeting domestic issues. As a result, legislative bills originate more and more with the executive. Presidential programs may be passed by the Congress, but they may be emptied of meaning, attenuated by self-seeking riders, or emasculated by inadequate funding. In many cases bills are restated in terms which place the onus for any unpopular results squarely on the executive—as, for example, in giving aid to communist countries or to those that have expropriated American property.

Fourth, it is impossible under the Constitution to bring the Executive and the Congress into harmony, because we lack strong and purposeful political parties. The Framers deplored political parties, which they called factions. As the political parties developed they were doomed to be mere alliances of State and local interests, because the Constitution allowed the States to determine the qualifications of voters and permitted the States to gerrymander the House districts to suit themselves. Indeed, the Constitution originally provided that Senators would be chosen by the Legislatures of the States, and it was not until the 17th Amendment was ratified in 1913 that Senators were elected by the people. The Framers provided that in each State the members of the Electoral College should be appointed in such "manner as the Legislature thereof may direct." The intention may or may not have been that the Legislatures would themselves appoint the members. When the electors finally came to be chosen by popular vote, it was still possible for local pressures to persuade them to refuse to vote for the party's candidate for President—which they sometimes do even yet.

The President must be a man of strong character and popular with the people if he is to be more than a figurehead in party leadership. His program of legislation cannot be passed unless he enjoys the good will, or at least the tolerance, of Congressmen of his own party and some of those in the opposition. Even then a second-term President may find his influence waning, and Congress may go its separate way, to the detriment of the nation's business and the citizens' welfare.

The opposition party, incidentally, fares even worse. Its defeated candidate has no power and, even in the unlikely event that he retains a seat in Congress or returns to a gubernatorial chair, he is a minor figure seriously handicapped in the task of rebuilding his defeated party.

These obstacles to progress and effective government are either implicitly or explicitly written into the Constitution, and it is time that an interested public arouses itself to search for remedies.

Chapter 3

DIVIDED WE FALL

THE NON-VIABLE STATES

It is usually agreed that without its recognition of State sovereignty the Constitution would never have won adoption. Just what the alternative might have been, we shall never know. Possibly some of the larger States would have absorbed their lesser neighbors, and there would have been four or five nations instead of one; possibly some of the States would have returned to the British allegiance, as Vermont seriously considered doing in the 1780's. But the fact was then and ever since has been that the States were not created by the historical interaction of geographical, cultural, linguistic, and political factors, as were, for example, England, France, and Spain.

On the contrary, most of the original thirteen colonies were founded by royal grants to trading companies and to "proprietaries" interested in selling land to religious refugees—or to anyone else who had the price. After independence, Congress whacked States out of the wilderness with, in general, what now seems a fine disregard of their chances of attaining viability. In fact, there was no good way that Congress could have done much better, since it had no means of knowing how the States would or could develop. For example, river transportation figured somewhat in the creation of the States east of the Great Plains because they were set up before the day of the railroad. Congress might have paid more attention to climatic zones and mountain divides, but perhaps it lacked information. Anyhow, there was a feeling that the new States should not be too large, lest the representatives of the people find it difficult to travel great distances to the capitals.

At any rate, the States never were viable economic entities even in the days when life was simpler and communities more nearly self-sustaining. Indeed, few of them have even been *politically* viable, as witness the political factions founded on geography in New York, Pennsylvania, Virginia, and California, to name only some of the most important.

The case for the absolute sovereignty of the States was extinguished by the Civil War, but even before that the champions of State sovereignty were obstructive rather than constructive. Frank Owsley, the Southern historian, goes so far as to say that the South failed to win independence chiefly because the component States insisted on their rights so vigorously as to thwart the military and economic measures of the Confederate government.

With the above facts in mind, it seems paradoxical that there should be so much state pride. In the words of the King of Siam, "It is a puzzlement." One is reminded of an anecdote that comes down from antebellum times. A re-survey of the boundary between Georgia and Alabama had resulted in putting a Georgia cracker family's cabin on the Alabama side of the line. No sooner had the matriarch of the family become aware of the fact than she gathered her brood about her and announced that they were moving.

"But what fer, ma?" protested the eldest son.

"Because thar's too much fever and agger in Alabamy," replied the old woman, "and I don't intend for you 'uns to catch it."

The variety of State systems has often been defended as a fruitful means of experimentation, and doubtless it is often so. On the other hand, if there were fewer States, their experiments might well be more visible and attract more effective public attention. As it is, whatever is of value in State experimentation is likely to be swamped in the public mind by a welter of political controversies. V. O. Key, Jr.[1] commented with some acerbity on the varieties of State political systems. Political parties perform essential functions in legislation, administration, and in keeping watch on each other, but they are more effective nationally than in the States. Some States do have effective rivalry between well-organized and sometimes well-led parties, but more commonly a single party dominates the government of the State. In this case, the real political struggle is between factions within the dominant political party. A national figure—even a President—interferes in these internecine combats only at his peril.

Woodrow Wilson pointed out at the beginning of the century that the encroachment of the Federal government on State powers was simply the filling of a vacuum—the States were not giving the public proper service. The fundamental reason, of course, was and is the lack of viability noted above, though there are other reasons, such as rigid constitutions, standpat legislatures, and inequitable

---

[1] *Politics, Parties, and Pressure Groups* (New York: Crowell, 1969), pages 283-284.

division of taxing powers. At any rate, Federal centralization has grown to an alarming extent, but it seems impossible to get agreement on what to do about it, though there is a considerable body of opinion that the powers of the States should be "restored." Unfortunately, in most instances the States never even pretended to exercise the powers which the dissidents now wish to have "restored" to them. It has been the Federal government which has heard the demand that public services be broadened to keep pace with the growing complexity of modern life, and has wheedled—some say seduced and bribed—the States into furnishing them by grants-in-aid and dollar matching.

The persistence of the cry against Federal "interference" is remarkable in view of the fact that the States have no real viability, are bogged down by antediluvian constitutions, hopelessly fragmented and expensive local governments, and systems of taxation that are universally on the verge of breakdown. Indeed, close examination reveals that these cries come from Neanderthal elements that seemingly aim at nothing less than the abandonment by both States and nation of many functions the public has come to regard as essential to its welfare. On the other hand, the minority elements that despair of justice at the hands of the ruling party are quite likely to appeal to Washington, a tendency encouraged by the way economic power has been gravitating into the hands of Congress, the President, and the Federal bureaucracy.

Despite this, the average citizen sees far more of his State and local government than of Federal officials. Indeed, most of the time the States manage to rock along fairly well. Their inability to act decisively—or perhaps justly—is exposed only when a crisis develops, as for example in labor relations, unemployment, race conflict, or inflation.[2]

The States are so disparate in population that this may well be one reason for the persistence of the claim to sovereignty made by those with smaller populations. Compare the 1970 population of Delaware (543,000) with that of its next-door neighbor, Pennsylvania (11.66 million); or that of Nevada (482,000) with California (19.7 million). The smaller States are afraid of being overshadowed by their larger neighbors and of losing their power of self-determination—this has actually occurred in the case of Nevada vis-à-vis California. Under such conditions it will certainly be difficult to persuade the states to consolidate into larger and more viable units, though this is perfectly legal under Article IV, Section 3, of the Constitution of 1787.

One element in the States' lack of viability is the antiquity of their constitutions, which in 1960 had an average age of about 83 years, including even Alaska and Hawaii, which had just been admitted. The constitution of Massachusetts was adopted in 1780, and in 1967 eighteen constitutions were over a century old.

---

[2]For more expansive treatments of these conditions, see again V. O. Key, *Politics, Parties, and Pressure Groups,* and York Wilbern, "The States as Components in an Areal Division of Powers," in Arthur Maass, ed., *Area and Power: A Theory of Local Government* (Glencoe, Ill.: The Free Press, 1959), pages 70-88.

Instead of periodically revising their constitutions to fit the times, the States typically adopt amendments. According to statistics compiled in 1967, the California constitution, adopted in 1879, had 350 amendments, and the Louisiana constitution, adopted in 1921, had 460 amendments and 236,000 words—well over three times the length of this book. Obviously much of the space is taken up by provisions that do not belong in any constitution—as, for example, California's prohibition of taxing nut trees under four years of age!

Another reason for the States' lack of viability is the fact that historically the rural localities and the legislatures have very often refused to adopt constitutions that permit executives to wield the power essential to efficiency and economy. This condition is still so prevalent that State governors and legislatures work under many of the same handicaps as do the President and Congress. Many State administrative officials are popularly elected, so that they owe little to the governor, and often do not even bother to consult him. As one political scientist has expressed it, the governor is merely the leading member of the executive department. He is not even the captain of a team, but only the titular head of a disparate group.

THE COMPLEXITY OF LOCAL GOVERNMENT

In considering the complexities of State and local governments, one is often puzzled over which has done the most to complicate the other. Jeffersonians wanted to keep governmental powers as nearly as possible in the hands of the people, but there has been a long struggle between localities and States over which should exercise certain powers. Today we see the States reluctant to grant adequate self-governing and taxing powers to the cities, with the result that the latter are rapidly becoming ungovernable.

But first let us turn to a short overview of local governments. The Bureau of the Census showed the following breakdown of local governmental units in 1967.

Counties	3,049
Municipalities	18,048
Towns and townships	17,105
School districts	21,782
Special districts	21,264
Total	81,248

Special districts included (among others) organizations to care for highways, cemeteries, fire protection, hospitals, housing, libraries, parks, sewers, and water. All together, 521,758 officials were elected. Local governments employed 6,539,000, of whom 4,550,000 were in education. The States employed 2,335,000 and the Federal government 2,993,000, besides those in the armed services. The grand total was 11,867,000 civilians, and with the armed services added, this put about 8 percent of the population on public payrolls—constituting, together with their dependents, perhaps as much as a quarter of the country's population. Even the table above shows a remarkable change from 1942, when there were 165,062 units; one might draw from this the implication that there is still hope.

It hardly need be said that a large proportion of these units of government have no good reason for existing separately but are an arrant waste of taxpayers' money. Counties furnish an illuminating illustration. Most counties east of the Rockies and in the Pacific Coast States were demarcated so that a farmer or stockman could ride in one day to the county seat, transact his business, and get back home in time to do his chores. This meant that in the typical county no citizen lived more than fifteen or twenty miles from the county seat. Though the automobile, hard-surfaced roads, and the telephone have long since rendered these demarcations obsolete, rigid State constitutions, added to a certain rural county pride and, even more important, entrenched and parasitical "courthouse gangs," have made it impossible to amalgamate groups of counties into larger and more economical and efficient units.[3]

De Tocqueville, in the 1830's, praised the American system of local government on the ground that the citizen took lessons "in the forms of governing from governing. The great work of society is ever going on before his eyes and, as it were, under his hands." Yet obviously many of the officials serve only part time ("sundown" civil servants) and receive little compensation. The result is that local government takes on a certain casualness, and teaches not how to govern but how not to govern. Certain offices become the private property of a family—as in one town in Vermont where five generations of the same family served as town clerks. The perquisites of local squires and constables are well known. Then there are times when an unsatisfactory person is kept on the public payroll simply to keep him off poor relief.

A serious problem is that in many States the present county and municipal forms of organization are sanctified by long usage or are written into the State constitutions and, for reasons already stated, are impervious to reform. Thus in northern Michigan and Wisconsin, where soil and climate conspire against profitable farming but timber and mineral resources once supported thriving counties, the counties limp on and on, despite the fact that the timber and minerals have been depleted. The western half of Texas—that is, west of 99°—is divided into 125 counties, which in that flat land, where travel is rapid, could easily be consolidated into 6 or 8, formed around that number of existing market towns. Consolidation of counties has been studied in perhaps forty States, and many proposals made. Here are a few examples:

---

[3]For a graphic description of how courthouse gangs operate, turn to Lane W. Lancaster, *Government in Rural America* (New York: D. Van Nostrand, 1952), and to Roscoe C. Martin, *Grass Roots* (University of Alabama Press, 1957). Between them, Lancaster and Martin effectively undermine the legend of grass-roots democracy.

State	Present number of counties	Reduce to
California	58	15
Kentucky	120	20
Nebraska	93	6
North Dakota	53	13
Oregon	36	7
Tennessee	97	12

In general, the States have a poor record in renovating local governments. Under the influence of rural legislators or of smaller cities, they refuse adequate governing and taxing powers to metropolitan centers. The tax base of core cities has declined disastrously as wealth has moved to the suburbs, and as blacks take over the cores they are as chary of cooperation with the white suburbs as the latter are distrustful of the cores. New York City is an example of a metropolis thus restricted; logically it should be joined with the adjacent urban areas of Connecticut and New Jersey to form a city-state. The "conurbations" that sprawl across State lines make it impossible for many of the present States to deal rationally with urban problems.

Just as bad is the way in which urban areas are hopelessly split among rival municipalities and tag ends of counties; in California, for example, Los Angeles and Orange Counties, with almost 8.5 million inhabitants in 1970, form one vast urban conglomerate. Yet in 1967 they held 100 separate municipalities and 344 other districts, all intermingled with non-contiguous fragments under county jurisdiction. Obviously, in these two counties there is a welter of jurisdictions—police, courts, school districts, zoning and planning regulations, waste and sewage disposal, sanitary regulation, street maintenance, building codes, and in some cases public utilities. As though this were not confusion enough, state highway and utility commissions often step in and make hash of whatever order the municipality has managed to create. The added tax burden imposed by such unrelated and uncooperative municipalities and districts is enormous, but nothing short of a dictatorial regime could force them to give up their precious independence. Unfortunately this stubbornness has been compounded by race antagonisms, not merely between whites on one side and black and Mexican-Americans on the other, but between blacks and Mexican-Americans.

CAN LOCAL GOVERNMENTS BE CONSOLIDATED?

Consolidation is not likely to work in either urban or rural areas unless the States yield the localities a greater measure of home rule. Nor does consolidation mean that the rural citizen would have to go to the county seat to transact *all* of his official business, for subsidiary offices could be located in convenient towns. Too, more use could be made of the device of giving large cities the status of counties; Virginia has tried this, though it has been far too generous in granting it to cities as small as 10,000.

Reorganization, it is clear, is no simple matter, for there is no demographic criterion that can be applied everywhere. [For example, Cook County, Illinois (Chicago) had 4.5 million inhabitants in 1950, while Armstrong County, South Dakota, had 42.] To quote glaringly obvious examples, the problem is quite different in an underdeveloped and all but uninhabited State like Alaska, a desert State like Nevada, and impacted States like Ohio and Rhode Island. The differences in taxable bases is equally obvious. Alaska and Nevada could never afford the public utilities, such as highways, that Ohio and Rhode Island could afford to finance without Federal aid if they really cared to.

Paul Ylvisaker has given a number of criteria for areal division of governmental powers, keeping in mind the need for serving the basic needs of society—liberty, equality, and service. Here we can give only his headings:

> MAXIM ONE: The areal division of powers should be concerned basically with what is meant by the phrase "the power to govern." The assignment of powers to component areas should in each case be a general one, covering the whole range of governmental functions [at that level], rather than a partial one related only to particular functions. . . .
>
> MAXIM TWO: The optimum number of levels among which to share the power to govern would seem to be three. . . .
>
> MAXIM THREE: The component areas should be constituted of a sufficient diversity of interests to ensure effective debate within each component and transcending communities of interest among the several components. . . .
>
> MAXIM FOUR: The components should not as such be represented in the legislatures of the higher levels. And it is an open question whether the areas of the components ought even to coincide with the legislative constituencies of the next higher level. . . .
>
> MAXIM FIVE: Four processes affecting intergovernmental relations should be provided for: one, a process of last resort to settle intergovernmental disputes and questions of jurisdiction; two, a process (or processes) of intergovernmental cooperation; three, a process by which the several governments may act separately and independently, as well as in cooperation; and four, a process of organic change which can neither be dictated nor stopped by a minority of components.[4]

The Federal government has sought to encourage neighboring municipalities to organize Councils of Government (COG) and give them power to administer area-wide problems. Thus far the municipalities have been more active in plan-

---

[4]Paul Ylvisaker, "Some Criteria for a 'Proper' Areal Division of Governmental Powers," in Arthur Maass, ed., *Area and Power: A Theory of Local Government* (Glencoe, Ill.: The Free Press, 1959), pages 34-39. Quoted by permission of the Macmillan Company.

ning than in performance, for the member units are reluctant to cooperate. Moreover, the fact that many impacted areas extend into the jurisdiction of two or more States makes cooperation difficult. Thus the problems of the District of Columbia can be successfully tackled only if Maryland and Virginia will permit the suburbs of Washington to cooperate with the city's COG. Here is an argument which should convince any reasonable Congressman that the District should be returned to Maryland; better yet, the adjacent parts of Virginia should be joined to the Washington metropolitan district and that should be under the jurisdiction, as I shall presently propose, of one State.[5]

CAN WE DECENTRALIZE?

The complexity of State and local governments is compounded by interstate relations and relations with the Federal government. There was argument in the First Congress in 1789 about entrusting the administration and enforcement of Federal laws to the States—such things as taxing, collecting customs duties, and trying judicial cases. Finally the Congress decided to set up Federal administrative and judicial apparatuses, but it did leave certain Federal matters to the States until it became convenient to take them over. If the Congress had made the contrary decision, it is barely possible that a rather different Federal system would have evolved, perhaps a system that would have muted the struggle over sovereignty.

Despite the omnipresence of the post office, internal revenue, and social security, the States—as already pointed out—still touch the daily life of the citizen more closely than does the Federal government. Indeed, the States seem to be increasing their contacts with the citizen. This increase, however, is due largely to the influence of the Federal government's encouragement of expanded civic services, as indicated before. It is not very fruitful to argue over the wisdom or folly of this influence, for it seems to be here to stay. Not only is big Federal government more aware of the needs of a modern society than the States but it is more sensitive to the social and economic needs of minorities—blacks, browns, and poor whites.

No one seems to be quite sure how many Federal programs there are giving grants-in-aid to the States and local entities, but there apparently are about 170. The problem is to introduce more efficiency into the expenditure of these funds. As a matter of fact, this is being done here and there as logical lines are drawn and confusion and duplication are reduced. For example, Congress has developed a formula for the distribution of highway funds that takes into consideration a

---

[5]The many publications of the Council of State Governments offer excellent analyses of state and urban problems.

State's area, rural population, and proportion of the national mileage of rural roads.

One way to reduce complexity would be to do away with duplicating bureaucracies. Most grants-in-aid, of course, carry guidelines which the States are supposed to follow, but it must be admitted that they are frequently neglected. Nevertheless, the system has swollen both the Federal and State bureaucracies, and there is a growing conviction even among liberals that it would be better all around if the guidelines were loosened—some of them even abandoned—and the States given more discretion in expending the grants. In effect this would be a partial institution of the scheme proposed in the First Congress to entrust the States with certain Federal functions.

Those who assume that Federal centralization is necessary to survival seem to me to be as far off the track as those who still quote Calhoun's defense of State sovereignty as the only defense of liberty. In my draft of the revised Constitution I name certain powers as falling within the province of the States, but also propose that Congress be empowered to set national guidelines which would govern the administration of these powers by the States. Moreover, it should be possible to turn certain Federal powers over to the States for administration. For example, why cannot Congress define all civil and criminal offenses, though leaving jurisdiction to the States? Original jurisdiction in most Federal cases should lie with the State courts, which should be able to call on other States to surrender fugitives, witnesses, and evidences, just as is now done under Federal warrants. I should like to point out here also that if the amending process is reasonably flexible, such experiments need not become irretrievably fixed.

There is much to be said for this decentralization, especially if the States would renovate their antiquated constitutions, tax structures, local governments, and bureaucracies. If the States could cooperate more whole-heartedly with each other in regional associations or authorities, they might well be entrusted with such present Federal functions as flood control, river navigation, forestry, agriculture, social security, medicare, small business loans, and perhaps administration of the public domain. As suggested in a previous chapter, it should remove many heated issues from Washington to the States, where they belong—as is the intention, for example, in India. The States should be better able than Washington to rehabilitate old cities and plan new ones, to solve social and racial problems, and to meet the problems of environmental pollution. The States should lift from the shoulders of Congressmen most of the burden of having to intercede with Washington bureaus on behalf of constituents whose social security checks have gone astray or who need other time-consuming services. Above all, decentralization should aid in the mitigating of State hostilities and competitiveness and promote formation of the regions of which I shall speak later. Even as it is, there were in 1966 some 144 active interstate compacts dealing with 21 matters, including such things as bridges, river clearance, forest fire protection, drivers' licenses, and exchange of indigents.

The foregoing analysis of Federal, State, and local problems and interrelation-
ships is cursory, but it does indicate some of the psychological, organizational,
and financial problems that are causing urban and rural decay and complicating
Federal and State administration. We can scarcely expect to find this confusion
suddenly ended, as happened (at least for the moment) in France when the
revolutionists cut through the medieval tangle and divided the country into
departements, arrondissements, cantons, and communes. But it should be possible to hammer constantly on the theme that government is unnecessarily duplica-
tive and expensive, and to keep the problems and the possible solutions
continually before the people. It is my hope and belief that if we can introduce
more flexibility into the Federal system and into the Federal government itself,
the example will encourage the States to tackle their own problems with more
imagination—and a considerable degree of ruthlessness.

I do not for a moment believe that we can intelligently draw up a final division
of powers between Federal and State governments—nor is there any reason to
assume that the framers of the Constitution thought they were doing that. We
cannot know the future movement of population and industry, nor can we know
what new cities and metropolitan areas will spring up nor which old cities will
become mere shells. We cannot foretell what new scientific advances will do to
agriculture, forests, or pasture lands, or what harvests the sea may bring forth.
There is even the possibility that human mistakes will melt the polar ice caps, with
the result that the climate will change drastically and coastal cities will be
submerged.

These are arguments against the preservation of State sovereignty as it now
exists and the preservation of the States as they now exist. But they are not
arguments against the rational division of powers (whether or not we call it a
division of sovereignty) between the nation and the States. In any case, they are
arguments against delay in beginning to consider how we can work our way out
of the quagmire in which we are caught and that threatens to suck us under. I
shall propose that we enter upon the decentralization of Federal functions and
the reorientation of Federal and State relations. Actually, this should not be as
difficult as it may seem at first glance. Even reasonable critics of centralization
quite often overlook the existence of a regionalism waiting to be summoned into
usefulness, a regionalism that can furnish not only the size appropriate to a
modern state but more of the necessary viability.

REGIONALISM: A HALF-WAY HOUSE

It is notable that such viability as the States have shown has been less in their
role of States than as parts of sections or regions. Frederick Jackson Turner, who
first sought to systematize the study of sections, stated flatly, "We in America are
in reality a federation of sections rather than of states," then added that "state
sovereignty has never been a vital issue except when a whole section stood behind

the challenging state." He further pointed out that when Congressional votes are charted on a map, "the areas of great geographic provinces are revealed by the map of votes." If this means anything, it means that the historic struggles over States' rights were in reality the attempts of sections to win autonomy or at the very least to act together in defense of their common interests. This is most clearly illustrated, of course, in the history of the South, but it appears also in New England, and less clearly in the Middle Atlantic States, the Border South, the Midwest, and the Pacific Far West.

The above facts suggest that, however inchoately it may have been expressed, there has always been a supra-state consciousness ready to assume a form and viability that the individual States have lacked. New England's sectionalism reached its acme at the Hartford Convention in 1814, and the South's sectionalism turned into Southern nationalism with secession.

The Civil War crushed Southern nationalism and assured that sectionalism would become a less self-assertive phenomenon—regionalism. Sectionalism had fostered cultural, social, and economic similarities in its component States and, at least in the case of the South, had looked toward independence. Regionalism shows some of the same similarities, but it does not aspire to independence, perhaps not even to common action. Rupert Vance pointed out long ago that a region is delineated by geography, culture, economics, and history, but that it also has internal diversities which mark sub-regions. The best test is probably the *feeling* of homogeneity which arises from psychological and historical factors, as well as from the generalized similarities in the other factors mentioned above. Howard Odum went a step further in defining sectionalism as "inbreeding" and regionalism as "line-breeding"—that is, readiness to absorb values and traits from outside.[6]

In the Far West, between the Rockies and the Pacific, regionalism is partly evidenced by a common historic feeling of *resentment* against the domination of San Francisco. As this shows, regional cooperation is sometimes more remarkable in the breach than in the observance. States occasionally unite for a limited specific purpose, there are regional governors' conferences, and private associations are formed to defend some cherished regional principle, as in the White Citizens Councils of the South. But attempts to organize regions into effective and permanent cooperating units have failed, except perhaps in the South. One reason is the rigidity of the Constitution, which recognizes no middle ground between the nation and the States. If any proof is needed it is seen in the fact that, instead of encouraging the States of the Tennessee Valley to cooperate in undertaking one of the most fruitful public enterprises ever known, the Federal Government did the job alone.

---

[6]See Rupert Vance, *Human Geography of the South* (1932); Howard Odum, *Southern Regions of the United States* (1936); and Howard Odum and Harry E. Moore, *American Regionalism: A Cultural-Historical Approach to National Integration* (1938), which exhaustively analyzes all aspects of regionalism for the 1930's and is still a mine of information and ideas despite the decline of railways and the rise of super-highways and skyways.

NEW STATES OF THE UNITED STATES
See maps No. 5 and No. 6

STATES	COMPONENTS	Approx. pop. 1970 in millions	Approx. no. Law Senators	Approx. no. Congressmen
ALASKA	Votes whether to become a Commonwealth or part of Oregon	.295		
ALLEGHENIA	Pa.; Del.; no. panhandle of W.Va.; N.J. so. of 40°18′; Md. east of Hancock; D.C.; Arlington, Fairfax, and Loudoun Counties, Va.	19.7	2 + 3	20
APPALACHIA	Ky. & Tenn. e. of Tenn. R.; Ala. no. of Tenn. R.; N.C.; Md. w. of Hancock; W.Va., except no. panhandle; Va., except Arlington, Fairfax, and Loudoun Counties	16.5	2 + 2	17
CALIFORNIA	From Pacific Ocean along no. line of San Luis Obispo Co.; to crest of Coast Range; to the Tehachapi Mts.; follow to Tehachapi Summit; thence w. to Colorado River and south to Mexico.	11.6	2 + 1	12
CHICAGO	From L. Mich. follow no. line to Ill. w. to 89° then so. to 41st par., east to 86° 45′; then no. to L. Michigan	8.	2	8
DESERET	Nev.; Utah; Ariz.; Colorado Basin part of Wyo.; Colo. & N.M. w. of Cont. Div., Sawatch, Sangre de Cristo and Sacramento Mts.; El Paso and Hudspeth Co's, Texas; parts of old Calif. not in new Calif. or Sierra	4.7	2	5
ERIE	Ohio; Ind. except Chicago area; Mich. except Upper Peninsula and tip given to Chicago	23.7	2 + 3	24
HAWAII	Unchanged	.748	2	1
MISSISSIPPI	Minn.; Iowa; Wisc.; Ill., except Chicago; N.E. Mo.; upper peninsula of Mich.	18.	2 + 3	18

NEW STATES OF THE UNITED STATES (Cont'd.)

STATES	COMPONENTS	Approx. pop. 1970 in millions	Approx. no. Law Senators	Approx. no. Con- gressmen
MISSOURI	N.D.; S.D.; Neb.; Kans.; Mont. & Wyo. e. of Cont. Div.; Colo. e. of Cont. Div., Sawatch & Sangre de Cristo Mts.; Mo. w. of 94° & No. of 37°	9.	2	9
NEW ENGLAND	Me.; N.H.; Vt.; Mass; R.I.; Conn. except Fairfield Co.; N.Y. north of 42°	16.	2 + 1	16
NEW YORK	N.Y. so. of 42°; Fairfield Co., Conn.; N.J. no. of 40° 18′	17.6	2 + 3	18
OREGON	Wash.; Ore.; Ida.; Mont. & Wyo. w. of Cont. Div.; Wyo. w. of Colo. R. Basin [and perhaps Alaska]	6.3	2	6
SAVANNA	S.C.; Ga.; Fla.; Ala., except part no. of Tenn. R.; Miss.; all of La. not in Texas; Ark. e. of 92°; Mo. e. of 92° and so. of 37°; Ky. & Tenn. w. of Tenn. R.	23.2	2 + 3	23
SIERRA	Follow present no. line of Calif. from Pacific to e. watershed of Sacramento R.; thence along crests of Sierra Nevada & Tehachapi Mts. to Coast Range; to no. line of San Luis Obispo Co.; and to the Pacific	8.2	2	8
TEXAS	Texas, except El Paso & Hudspeth Co.s; Okla.; N.M. east of Sangre de Cristo & Sacramento Mts.; Mo. so. of 37° and west of 92°; Ark. west of 92°; La. west of 92° and no. of 31°	15.	2 + 1	15
Total		198.748	50	200

The Census of 1970 gives a population of 200,251,000. The discrepancy above is due not only to the dropping of many uneven numbers but also to the unfeasibility of counting the populations of the fragments of counties divided between the new States. The population in each new State, therefore, can only be an approximation.

Chapter 4

A SCHEME FOR THE CONSOLIDATION OF STATES

CARVING OUT NEW STATES

When we begin to examine the feasibility of using regionalism as a means of decentralizing Federal functions and power, it is interesting to find that it has already begun after a fashion—but only after a fashion—with the removal of certain Federal bureaus from Washington to other parts of the country and the division of their functions among areas. What is needed is action (1) to establish officially a number of regions, organized as new States, and to assign to each the administration of those parts of the bureaucracy that concern it; and (2) to encourage the new States to cooperate in common enterprises, using their enlarged facilities and tax resources wherever their interests require common action.

This program inevitably will require revision of the Constitution of 1787, and there will be many differences of opinion about the forms the changes should take. My own belief is that we can dispense with the historical "sovereignty" of the States and substitute a flexible arrangement that will make it possible to alter borders as conditions change. The new States should not only retain control of matters of plainly local interest, but the Federal government should enable them to handle with more independence more functions than they do now. For example, after groups of States are consolidated and their Constitutions modernized, their courts could exercise original jurisdiction in cases involving most Federal laws. As has already been urged, under Federal guidelines they could handle many present Federal functions—perhaps river navigation, administration of public lands and parks, more areas of social action, and regulation of sanitation, pollution, and ecology.

34

Properly handled, such an arrangement would lift much of the burden from the President and Congress and put more of the political heat on the States, where it really belongs. Such new flexibility would also make it possible to experiment.

What standards should be used in carving out the regions that should be consolidated into new States? A host of possible guidelines come to mind, most immediately the climatic and physiographical, including mountains, plains, rivers, rainfall, soil, forests, and proximity to lake and sea ports. Then there are historical, ethnic, cultural, and urban factors. The problem is that many of these patterns—even climate and physiography—change with time. Indeed, the factors are interwoven so intricately that no one is foolproof, and that is a good reason why a revised Constitution should provide that the borders of regional States should never become sacrosanct, as are the present borders of States. Will new cities replace or supplement the mushrooming suburbs of the old? Will industry effectively be dispersed? Will financial controls be decentralized? Will the socialistic aspects of the mixed economy increase? Will the much-needed leveling off in population be realized? Conditions change too quickly and populations move too rapidly to permit us to say that the sparsely populated region of today will not be the most populous a century hence. Certainly we cannot hope to have States remain anywhere near equal in population even if they are set up that way at first, and so let us abandon that standard at once.

Still, the movement toward the amalgamation of States must begin somewhere. For this reason I have taken certain historic, climatic, and geographical factors that can be used as initial guides. These sometimes result in cutting across existing State lines, and I have acknowledged this with a candor that most readers will be inclined to regard as audacious, if not downright foolhardy.

The accompanying maps show (1) the principal river valleys and mountain watersheds; (2) the historical sections of the United States about 1820; (3) the historical sections of the United States about 1850–1900; (4) the more important metropolitan areas; (5) a scheme for the organization of regions into new States, giving the population in 1970 of each new State; and (6) a special map showing details of the proposal for consolidation of States in the Northeast. A special effort has been made to promote topographical unity and to unify the great conurbations either as separate States or within single States.

Now of course it is impossible to pitch on an optimum area or population for a region, and so uniformity in either cannot be a guide. Hawaii can probably meet the standard of viability better than most of the present States, but Alaska, which certainly cannot, should be given the choice of joining greater Oregon or becoming a Commonwealth, self-governing in every respect save for control of foreign affairs, defense, and administration of the public domain. As a Commonwealth its people would be citizens of the United States, protected by its Bill of Rights and Senate courts, entitled to share in Congressional welfare appropriations provided the guidelines are met, and exempt from Federal internal taxes under conditions set by Congress.

Puerto Rico is the thorniest problem. Probably it should be encouraged to declare complete independence, with the United States guaranteeing it certain trade favors for the next generation or so—but favors *to Puerto Ricans,* not to American enterprise.

It is just as impossible to see the Great Basin–Colorado River States coalescing with California, for their antipathy has run broad and deep for a century. Rivers ought to bind together the states on their banks, and this may be acceptable in the case of the Missouri River, but the Mississippi, the Ohio, and the Potomac have been historical dividing lines. (See Map 1 for river valleys.)

Mountain ridges have served as political boundaries throughout history, but in the United States they have lost much of their significance because of railroads, roads, and airplanes. There are points at which it becomes absurd to use watersheds as political dividing lines. The Appalachian divide, serrated by deeply piercing rivers, has never been used as a State boundary, and there is now even less reason so to use it. On the other hand, though the Continental Divide in the Far West is, over much of its way, a logical division, it has been used as a State boundary for only a short distance between Idaho and Montana. But even the Continental Divide is not always clear to the motorist; there are places in Wyoming and New Mexico where he knows he is crossing the Divide only because roadside signs inform him. Still, the Continental Divide should be used, except perhaps in Colorado and New Mexico, where the Sangre de Cristo and Sacramento Mountains afford a better alternative (See Map 5.)

Finally, but by no means least important, the States grouped together not only must have a reasonable degree of topographical, historical, cultural, and economic affinity but must not be widely separated in per capita wealth. This is the hardest standard of all to observe, but if the spread is too great and the richer states are the more populous, the poor states are likely to remain poor unless they can rely on Federal resources. A state may be poor not because of a low per capita income or assessed valuation, but because its area is large in proportion to its population, a condition that makes it difficult to form needed capital and furnish needed services. This can be seen particularly in the States composing the proposed States of Missouri, Oregon, and Deseret. Consequently, these standards cannot be followed slavishly. Nevertheless, the formation of Oregon and Deseret should enable the components of each to unite in a more efficient development of their resources, and it scarcely need be repeated that one purpose of this study is to find ways to decentralize power and enable the regions to handle their own affairs to the limit of their ability.

THE NORTH

We can now turn to the task of suggesting possible groupings of States into new States. Reference to Map Number 4 will show a great urban complex extending for over 400 miles from New Hampshire to northern Virginia, though at present its density thins out somewhat at the Housatonic River in Connecticut, in mid-New Jersey, and at the northern end of Chesapeake Bay. Washington's southern suburbs, which now extend for miles into Virginia, include well over 200,000 people, most of them dependent in one way or another on the Federal government. The existence of this 400-mile urban complex makes it very difficult to demarcate regions, for the greater segments, as noted above, cross state lines. Only less significant than New York are two other metropolitan areas: one extends from Pittsburgh to Detroit, and the other is at the southern end of Lake Michigan.

In an economic sense the North, from Boston to the Mississippi River, is the fulfillment of Alexander Hamilton's dream of an industrial empire: for a century and a half, a succession of ruthless practical dreamers fought against the opposing agrarian concepts in order to make Hamilton's dream come true.[1]

The result is that today New York and, to a lesser extent, Chicago wield, for good or evil, a financial and economic power never before matched. Today the Northeast and the Old Northwest or Middle West are in virtual alliance both economically and politically and may be lumped together as the North or the East. Until the 1930's the North was able to stack the cards in its favor—and to a considerable extent still is. The tariffs were written largely to favor industry. Corporations were the chief beneficiaries of tax rebates, and they were able at times to dragoon Federal and State governments into settling taxes for a fraction of the sums assessed. With some exceptions the great corporations are effectively controlled in the North, regardless of where their stockholders live. This is aptly illustrated not only by the great manufacturing corporations but by communications media and by the chains that now control so many drug, variety, grocery, and department stores.

Though it seems clear that the North's throttlehold on finance and industry was made possible only because of the historic community of interest among the bankers of Wall Street (the Street was shorn of most of its power by the New Deal), it is not likely that they either "conspired" or consciously sought to impose "tyranny" as such. Their motives were probably no more sinister than a single-minded and rather short-sighted search for profits. In this search they used many weapons to neutralize established competitors and to prevent the rise of new competitors, meanwhile mouthing and perhaps believing the shibboleths of free enterprise, laissez faire, competition, and the law of supply and demand. Businessmen point out, and justly, that they are largely responsible for the American standard of living and that this standard depends on concentration, efficiency, expensive experimentation, and the other factors that go to make mass production

[1]Much of the following material on the regions is drawn from my own *The Meaning of America* (University of Pittsburgh Press, 1955), Chapter 1.

possible. The North has furnished much of the capital and technical skills for the development of the rest of the country, and it has sometimes managed to appropriate the results even when local capital and initiative have built a business.

NEW ENGLAND

Of the parts into which the North falls, New England gives the impression of greatest antiquity—indeed it is often accused of being arid, meager, and decadent, a civilization which has been completed and has nothing more to say. It is true that the New England capitalists, managers, and technologists who did much to make America have passed on. Today Boston's "spendthrift" trusts sit on their millions, while the gadgeteers of Connecticut and Rhode Island turn to New York for inspiration. Inundations of immigrants—Irish, Slav, French-Canadian, and Latin—have swept over the area and altered its face and its religion but, strangely enough, have found an affinity for some aspects of its Puritanism. The French-Canadians, in fact, came from a culture dominated by Catholic Ultramontanism, which has certain resemblances to one side of Puritanism. New England remains what it always was, a dualism at once pragmatic and transcendental.

New England was a paradox from the first, and this is illustrated by the quip that the Pilgrim fathers fell first on their knees and then on the aborigines. New England still presents the paradox of democracy and cliques, of mediocre conformists and eccentric "againsters." Its towns may be primly beautiful or awesomely ugly. At one extreme Boston offers a boiling of Irishmen, Jews, Italians, Middle Yankees, and "Brahmins." The latter exhibit facets of ritualism, provincialism, and public spirit along with ruthless flouting of political and economic ideals that would be called cynical in a less self-assured city. At the other extreme Vermont is rural, canny, neighborly, individualistic—and completely self-assured. It is thus not strange that Vermont, an intensely democratic state that almost invariably goes Republican, gave America its leading Utopians, those zealous searchers for the City of God. There was significance in the decision of Vermont's first legislature "to adopt the laws of God . . . until there is time to frame better!"

The New England States are strangely diverse and yet strangely unified. The contrasting ethnic groups, cultures, and mores now simmering within its borders offer a sound basis for a rich future broth. However that may be, the historical influence of New England is beyond dispute. Its reformists left an indelible stamp on education, literature, and social welfare; its inventors laid the basis for mass production and the American standard of living; its canny traders, who knew how to take calculated risks, contributed significantly to making New York City a paramount commercial entrepot; its financiers and managers did much to give the country its magnificent transportation system; and its statesmen contributed mightily to the idea of nationhood.

Moving from the sawtooth mountains of New England across gangling Lake Champlain to the colorful, lake-gemmed Adirondacks, one enters the so-called Middle Atlantic States. New York is as rich in history and natural wonders as any State in the Union, and as paradoxical as New England, though in a different way. Its upper stretch, though highly industrialized, preserves many of the conservative traits of its New England settlers and long imposed upon New York City (which almost doubles it in population) a position of inferiority in the councils of the State. Thus I am inclined to claim that upper New York should be a part of New England by virtue of its settlers and its political and social traits being New England in origin.

NEW YORK CITY

New York City and the adjacent areas of Connecticut and New Jersey should be set up as a city-state. That New York City is a giant needs no emphasis here. It may not be the world's largest incorporated city but, with the adjacent "bedroom towns" of New Jersey and Connecticut, it is the center of the most populous metropolitan area in the United States, with about 17 million people. It leads in commerce, in finance, and in industrial production. Its budget is larger than that of most States and most nations. It is the cultural capital of America (it would fain assert of the world): at least it leads the United States in publishing, art, music, opera, ballet, and the theater—Hollywood is merely a convenient "shooting" location a short hop from Forty-Second Street. It is the clearing house for news and opinion. It leads in styles, fads, and the argot of the underworld. As the Vanity Fair of the entertainment world, the nexus of luxurious hotels and restaurants, and the center of universities, libraries, museums, art galleries, and laboratories, it teems with playboys, gourmets, dilettantes, scholars, and scientists. It abounds in bridges, boulevards, skyscrapers, penthouses, slums, and bathing beaches, all on a commendably colossal scale.

And it is ungovernable—at least under present institutional conditions. Its population is polyglot: it has more Negroes and more Jews than any other city in the world; more Irish than any other city except Dublin; more Italians than —fill it in for yourself; and not least of all it probably has more Americans born somewhere else than any other city except Los Angeles. Its people are surging, intense, callous, supercilious, provincial beneath a shell of sophistication, and obsessed with a craze for money and high living—a craze not restricted to New Yorkers or to Americans. Religious, racial and ideological rivalries are always on tap, for New York City, with its abortive Americanism, combines the most raucous Europeanism and Africanism. The rest of the country regards New York with an amusing mixture of awe, admiration, contempt, envy, and resentment— all well justified. The accusation is made that New York City is more parasite and dictator than reflector of American attitudes, and so there is resentment that it should presume to act as spokesman for the country. William Allen White complained that New York would take God himself on its knee and tell him the facts of life.

ALLEGHENIA

Across the Hudson River lies New Jersey, a bedroom, coast resort, and vegetable patch for New York and Philadelphia, and a manufacturing center in its own right. Philadelphia, oozing history from every pore, prosperous with its sprawling industries—a city which until quite recently seemed to have lost the civic consciousness of Franklin and Rush but preserved the snobbishness that once caused its social leaders to cross the street to avoid speaking to that arch-radical, Vice-President Thomas Jefferson. To the north of it lie the anthracite coal fields, to the west the rich agricultural lands of the Pennsylvania Germans; beyond the Susquehanna are forests that, paradoxically, are teeming with deer and bears. Among the mountains and west of them are coal and steel centered on Pittsburgh, a city of blackened spires and homes, vigorous, rough as its mill hands, with the spiritual rigidity of its Presbyterian founders.

In the old days the Mason and Dixon line (see Map 2) was the southern boundary of the imperial North, but industry has encroached upon the South. Delaware's once sleepy fields are now the home of vast enterprises in munitions, chemicals, and nylons, spearheads of a mushrooming Du Pont empire. The Free State of Maryland, once a planting colony cleft by Chesapeake, is now divided as sharply between industrial Baltimore and farmers and fishermen, while an enclave of Maryland soil has become the District of Columbia, the center of a million and a quarter inhabitants, mostly government workers, their families, and their suppliers. The above areas could be joined to Pennsylvania in a new State (to be called *Alleghenia*) formed by uniting the northern panhandle of West Virginia, southern New Jersey, Maryland east of Hancock, Delaware, the District of Columbia and, to give Washington a chance to organize a rational city government, the three adjacent counties of Virginia.

THE MIDDLE WEST

The Old Northwest—the area between the Mississippi and Ohio rivers— became known as the Middle West after the rise of the Great Plains West, and the name has stuck, though it is no longer appropriate. There is no foolproof way of defining the Middle West, but one may cautiously affirm that it includes those States in the sphere of influence of Chicago in which there is a fair balance between industry and agriculture—the marriage of machine tools and Corn Belt. This would include not only the original five but Minnesota, Iowa, Missouri, and possibly Kentucky. The five States of the Old Northwest came closest in the

North, after New England, to meeting the definition of a region. Set apart by Congress in 1784, they found common ties in free farming, the corn-hog cycle (except in Wisconsin and Michigan), and finally in manufacturing—not to mention sharing a common commercial and financial center in Chicago. True, the Old Northwest was predominantly settled along the Ohio by Southern Highlanders, in the north by New Englanders, and in between by Alleghenians and a mixture from other areas; but they eventually coalesced to form the political and industrial heart of America—indeed, its cultural heart, also, and even the dialect known, whether or not correctly, as General American.

The mechanical bent of the Middle West probably came not only from Yankee artisans but from immigrant Germans and from the so-called Pennsylvania Dutch. No section, not even the Northeast, has enjoyed such good transportation, for not only are there rivers and lakes, but the terrain lends itself to railroad and highway building. Timber and minerals have been abundant and easily accessible, and the States favored entrepreneurs from the first. In no other section have public schools and State universities played such an important role, nor State and county fairs.

Few dispute that the Middle West is the heart of American physical and moral strength. It is, moreover, the epitome of the American mythus at its best and worst. There we see enlightened industrialists—and ruthless oppressors; militant and responsible labor leadership—and labor racketeers; tolerant and socially conscious churches—and cheap, emotional, anti-intellectual preachers of fear; courageous, responsible, and intelligent social and political leadership—and sowers of seeds of hatred. The area is often called the "Valley of Democracy," and indeed it does show democracy in successful action—but also the political machine at its most cynical. No other section of the country witnesses more desperate political battles nor ones in which the forces are better balanced. There is a saying: "We haven't made up our minds which side we're on, but when we do you can be sure we'll be damned bitter about it."

The nucleus of this vast region is Chicago, a metropolitan center of 8,000,000 people, blessed with an incomparable geographic position and cursed with extremes of weather—the temperature can fall forty degrees in an hour. Behind a magnificent lake front stretches a flat, humdrum waste of drab dwellings, factories, and railroad tracks. Based on railways, steel, manufacture of agricultural machinery and countless other articles, and retailing (consider its amazing mail order houses), it holds an impregnable economic position. Filled with foreign-born of all nations, it is yet more typically American than New York—and seemingly determined to match every characteristic with a paradox.

The Middle West has been called the home of dead-level, democratic mediocrity, yet its States each show character. Ohio has long been a meeting ground of cultures—easternmost of the Western States, westernmost of the Eastern, and northernmost of the Southern. Here have met New England reformism, Western individualism, and Southern localism to make it a political swing state—hence the numerous Presidential candidates chosen from Ohio, and the seven Presidents born in or elected from Ohio who have given it the title Mother of Presidents. (It may or may not be significant that all of them have been Republicans and none of them has been outstanding.) Ohio's urbanism is pronounced and its cities are among the most civically and culturally conscious in the country. On the other hand, its farmers are united and highly vocal and constitute the State's largest pressure group.

Indiana has a balance between industry and agriculture, but is popularly regarded as rural, perhaps because of James Whitcomb Riley's popular "When the Frost Is on the Punkin." Local patriotism is high in Indiana, and its citizens are perpetually bathed in a mellow sentimental glow. Nevertheless, its mores are shrewd and conservative and its politics bitterly contested. Though its intelligentsia tend to migrate, they never lose their nostalgia for the moonlight on the Wabash.

There remain the States that not only front on the Great Lakes but depend more vitally on them as arteries of transport. They were in great part the creation of New Englanders, Germans, and Scandinavians. Wisconsin, long the home of a third party, the Progressive, boasts of its industry. Michigan, with chemical industries, iron ore, copper, and timber slashings, now finds its mission chiefly in the automobile industry of the Detroit area. This industry, long notoriously anti-labor in its policies (perhaps partly because it was so sensitive to the national economic temperature), has attracted not only Negroes and immigrants—chiefly Poles—but great numbers of volatile and race-conscious white Southerners. The result has been the mushrooming of a city that rivals Chicago in its vigorous and brutal materialism and exceeds it in explosive possibilities.

Though it may legitimately claim to be a region, yet with 40 million people the Middle West is simply too enormous to be organized as one State. Then there is the Chicago area which, with its 8 million people, tyrannizes over Illinois, and similar metropolises may well emerge in southern Michigan and northern Ohio —but not yet. Accordingly I propose to set Chicago aside as a city-state; to join Ohio, Indiana, and Lower Michigan as the State of *Erie;* and to join Minnesota, Wisconsin, the Upper Peninsula of Michigan, Iowa, Illinois, outside Chicago, and most of Missouri as the State of *Mississippi.*

The present state of Missouri is a Southern State with northern and western exposures, and so is the odd State in the last combination, but from St. Louis northward it is quite compatible with Iowa and Illinois, despite the "Little Dixie" area between the Missouri and Mississippi Rivers and adjoining Illinois. I suggest that Missouri be divided horizontally at 37° which would put most of the Missouri River's tributaries in the new State of *Mississippi,* and leave the southern counties to be divided between the proposed States of *Savanna* and *Texas.* I have also proposed that Missouri be divided vertically at the 94th meridian in order to place the entire metropolitan district of Kansas City in a new and greater State of *Missouri* which I shall later describe.

THE ENDURING SOUTH

No section has been so persistently misrepresented as the South—and with such bland inconsistency—by the rest of the American people. At one extreme there is the traditional "Dixieland," with its pillared mansions, dancing "darkies," moonlight and honeysuckle, unexcelled cooking, and unlimited hospitality generously spiked with mint juleps or bourbon and branch water. At the other extreme is the land of the frying pan cuisine, a country of merciless sun and rain, infested with cottonmouth moccasins, no less poisonous demagogues, moldy aristocrats, and shoeless sharecroppers whose only vitality comes with the kick of the white mule and the community summons to share in the regional sport of burning Negroes. There is a third mythus—the Southerner's impression of himself.

Needless to say, all three pictures are some distance from the truth, yet there has been some truth in each of them. Hence the Southern paradox, which is in type also the American paradox. Still, there is about the South a certain mystique that is not present in the North. Perhaps the poet caught something of this when he told of Wingate, a Confederate soldier, brooding on the causes of the Civil War.

> It wasn't slavery,
> That stale red-herring of Yankee knavery
> Nor even states-rights, at least not solely,
> But something so dim that it must be holy.
> A voice, a fragrance, a taste of wine,
> A face half-seen in old candleshine,
> A yellow river, a blowing dust,
> Something beyond you that you must trust,
> Something so shrouded it must be great,
> The dead men building the living State
> From 'simmon-seed on a sandy bottom
> The woman South in her rivers laving
> That body whiter than new-blown cotton
> And savage and sweet as wild-orange-blossom,
> The dark hair streams on the barbarous bosom,
> If there ever has been a land worth saving—
> *In Dixie land, I'll take my stand,*
> *And live and die for Dixie!*[2]

---

[2]Stephen Vincent Benét, *John Brown's Body*. (Holt, Rinehart and Winston, Inc.) Copyright 1927, 1928 by Stephen Vincent Benét. Copyright renewed 1955, 1956 by Rosemary Carr Benét. Reprinted by permission of Brandt and Brandt.

One of the most remarkable aspects of American history is the continued vitality of the South. As early as 1750 its peculiar planter economy seemed doomed to disappear before the small farmer, but the Industrial Revolution gave cotton (and with it slavery) a stimulus that renewed the life of the planter economy. When once more *it* seemed about to fall, this time before the onslaught of its creator, the Industrial Revolution, Northern ineptitude and the exacerbation of race antipathies gave it even in defeat a new psychological life that insured its immortality as a separate region even more certainly than its planter economy had in the old days. Under the leadership of its "Bourbon brigadiers," the defeated South drew together as a tight garrison devoted to the defense of its ideals. It yielded economic control to the North in the so-called "Treaty of 1877" in order to preserve the central values of aristo-agrarianism and white supremacy.

Thereafter its internal politics were devoted to maintaining discipline in the Southern garrison, and its external politics to the search for a means of vetoing those national policies which it regarded as inimical to its two cherished interests. The South blamed the Republican Party for the Civil War, and so it gave its allegiance to the Democratic Party. Thereafter for half a century the Solid South was a significant factor in the threshing out of American policies. Even when in later years its solidarity has been seriously breached in Presidential elections, it has remained stubbornly Democratic in local government.

The old rivalry of Massachusetts and Virginia for national ascendance has come down to us. Massachusetts has made this an industrial nation, has placed its stamp on the newer regions to the west, and has even made deep inroads into the Texas-Southwest and into the South itself—but the South has built a psychological ark upon which it resists the attempts of Massachusetts to lay its profane hands.

The South is rich in material and human resources but lagging in capital wealth, in technology, and in the institutions that bring together the other factors to create a satisfactory society. The South therefore is a land where human and material resources are wasted, where imbalances reign in culture and economy, and where old fears and prejudices are sometimes more powerful than scientific facts. The blame can fall upon the South only in part, for it has been the victim (as well as in some respects the beneficiary) of an expanding economy—the aphis to the industrial ant. The Bourbon brigadiers made their "Treaty of 1877" with the North on terms that seemed most likely to preserve the way of life which they and the South treasured; in other words, they sought to preserve the very status of agricultural and social imbalance that now is accused of being at the core of the modern South's difficulties.

The South is still rural and conservative in its outlook, even in' some of the cities, and is tinctured everywhere with the paternalism that accompanied the older planter economy. Family ties are strong, and the traditional regard for religion is still potent. Part and parcel of this attitude is the Southerner's supreme race-consciousness, what Odum calls the Southern Credo—the belief that the

Negro "could not be expected ever to measure up to the white man's standard of character and achievement." Nevertheless, the South has had a long history of liberalism, and it is possible to show that it swings back and forth with the rest of the country. This tendency is concealed by the fact that until recently it was always Democratic; when the country went conservative Republican, the South merely supported conservative Democrats.

It must not be supposed that the black population of the South outnumbers the white except in limited areas. Indeed, in slavery times in the slave states as a whole, only about a quarter of the white families owned even one slave. The proportion of slaves was even smaller in the mountains, for over considerable areas a black face was a rare and amazing sight. Indeed, it may be fair to say that the Border States and the Deep South were different not merely because of climate and topography but because the greater number of Negroes in the latter increased white solidarity even among the yeoman farmers and poor whites.

Of all the regions of the United States, the South has probably been the most homogeneous—not racially, but in the white man's nostalgia for the Lost Cause. This does not mean that its economic pattern is the same everywhere, beyond the fact that until recently about three-fourths of its people were engaged in agriculture. Even its agriculture follows no definite pattern. Virginia, North Carolina, Tennessee, and Arkansas engage in general farming and tobacco growing, with the latter two growing some cotton. The cotton belt, from South Carolina to Texas, produces increasing amounts of other crops. Georgia has peach and pecan orchards, Florida citrus groves and truck gardens, and Louisiana sugar and rice. Its manufactures are chiefly cotton textiles and products and steel and wood products, with some shipbuilding thrown in. One noticeable fact is that the South is still dependent on the North for machine tools, and so does not possess the ability to renew itself. The largest metropolitan area in the "Deep South" is Atlanta, with upwards of 1.25 million people. It has the best claim to be called regional capital, but even this claim remains to be proved. New York and Chicago are still the queen cities of the South.

APPALACHIA AND SAVANNA

Southern homogeneity, it should be emphasized, is not racial or economic but psychological. As a matter of fact, there are numerous minor sub-regions in the South, each with its own economic interests and view of history. For purposes of this reorganization I have undertaken to stress the three most significant sub-regions: the Border or Upper South, which I have called *Appalachia;* the Deep South, which I have called *Savanna;* and certain parts of Missouri, Arkansas, and Louisiana that look westward toward eastern Oklahoma and Texas; these I propose be joined to a Southern Plains State to be called *Texas,* which I will leave for later treatment.

Appalachia, as I propose it, would consist of Virginia (except for three counties), Maryland west of Hancock, West Virginia (except for the northern panhandle), North Carolina, Kentucky and Tennessee east of the Tennessee River, and the part of Alabama north of the Tennessee.

Antebellum Virginia west of the Blue Ridge Mountains possessed few slaves, took little interest in Southernism, and chafed under unprogressive Tidewater Virginia's discriminatory taxation and refusal to give it adequate legislative representation. A group of westerners led by Wheeling businessmen was interested in the Baltimore and Ohio Railroad and wished to win free of Tidewater in order to exploit the coal and timber in the mountain region. The Civil War gave them their opportunity. With Lincoln's backing, they set up a loyal governor and legislature, and this "restored Virginia" authorized the separation of West Virginia, which Congress admitted to the Union in 1863. West Virginia held undisputed possession only of the northern counties, for most of the present State, even though occupied by Union troops, was bitterly secessionist or at least opposed to the creation of a new State. But the Wheeling businessmen and their allies had what they wanted, and during the next generation gutted the State of its resources and left it all but pauperized.

But most of West Virginia preserves its character as a part of the Upper South; the chief exception is the northern panhandle. Virginia, West Virginia, and Kentucky were once all part of the same State, and North Carolina and Tennessee were once one State; indeed, the Virginia Grant of 1609 included North Carolina, so that the region historically could be called Virginia. These five States meet fairly well the definition of a region. The Appalachian Mountains cover two-thirds of the area, the original home of the Southern Highlanders, who were prominent in the westward movement and who still form the majority culture in the homeland. Even the "romantic" aristocrats of Tidewater Virginia were never as numerous as their yeoman farmer neighbors in the Piedmont, though they did manage to lend a tinge to lowland Kentucky. The mountains no longer function as separating walls, for railroads, turnpikes, and airplanes pass them easily and unite two great areas in which the people are related by blood and culture.

The Deep South consists essentially of the Gulf Plain, which I here call Savanna, though most of the area was included in the Carolina Grant of 1663 and hence historically could be called Carolina. Properly speaking, a savanna is a grassy plain, but much of the Deep South was given over to various kinds of pine woods. However, there were savannas along the east and south coasts, over most of Florida, and in the so-called Black Belt of fertile black prairie in Alabama and Mississippi. The clearing of the inland forests has turned much more of the Gulf Plain into savanna-like country. The Deep South, except for Florida and other parts of the Gulf coast, found a common interest in cotton culture, and the Cotton Kingdom also extended into Texas and up the Mississippi shores of Arkansas, Tennessee, Kentucky, and part of Missouri. For this reason I would extend Savannah northward along the Mississippi as far as Cairo, would add to it the parts of Kentucky and Tennessee west of the Tennessee River, and would omit the area of Alabama north of the Tennessee.

THE GREAT WEST

No real American can think of the West without feeling a nostalgic pang for the days—mostly legendary—when men were ruggedly individualistic. Here is the explanation of the perennial popularity of the Western novel and moving picture, of the small boy's craze for cowboy togs. The West brings before our mind's eye a sweeping panorama: the towering Rockies, the mighty Columbia; hills clothed with giant redwoods and Douglas firs; vast pasturelands; fertile, secluded valleys; gold placers, and silver and copper mines; sunny haciendas, white beaches, the blue Pacific; and, perhaps most vividly of all, the Southwestern desert, which Bob Beverley calls "the land that seems to be grieving over something—a kind of sadness, loneliness in a deathly quiet." We are in love with solitude, with the ideal of the strong, silent, self-reliant man of Western legend.

> The West itself is the place where you climb for water, dig for wood, look farther and see less, and the Powder River runs uphill from Texas. It's a land of fable, myth, tradition and the lack of it, extremes of heat and cold, wetness and dryness, lowness and highness, of promise and bitter disappointment, of million-dollar schemes by the countless people who own no more than a jalopy or the down-payment on a radio. It's a land that has been exploited worse than almost any other part of the globe; and a land still incredibly rich in resources, in plans, hopes, and eagerness to find a "pardner" who will grubstake a "deal."[3]

The States of the West have certain problems in common: (1) they are colonial areas subject to Northern financial and sales exploitation, and they claim that they suffer from unreasonable freight rates and other deliberate discouragements to industry; (2) great areas within the borders of most of the States are owned by the Federal government and are either withheld from use or carefully supervised in their use; (3) many of the States depend on Federal bounty to maintain essential public services; (4) they have a common Jeffersonian tradition, with its deeply implanted suspicion of government; and (5) there is an all but general lack of easily available water except in the States adjacent to the Mississippi—and sometimes even there.

Obviously the Great West offers a problem when one begins to consider the consolidation of States, and so as a first step I have ventured to divide the problem

---

[3]Ladd Haystead, *If the Prospect Pleases: The West the Guidebooks Never Mention* (University of Oklahoma Press, copyright 1945), pages 7-8. Quoted by permission of the University of Oklahoma Press.

into two parts by drawing a line along the Continental Divide from the Canadian boundary southward to the lower end of the Sawatch Range in Colorado and then along the Sangre de Cristo and Sacramento Mountains to the Rio Grande. We can give first consideration to the States of the Great Plains.

A GREATER MISSOURI AND A GREATER TEXAS

Walter P. Webb, in *The Great Plains,* included in his area everything from the 98th meridian to the Pacific Ocean, with a serrated extension to the eastward reaching through Illinois and into Indiana. Of course he knew that the 98th meridian is not an accurate dividing line between adequate rainfall and the semi-arid plains, and he recognized that mountains and deserts are interspersed farther west. But he did find considerable climatic and biological similarity in the "Great Plains Environment" and graphically described the roles of the revolver, the barbed wire fence, and the windmill in the conquest of the area. Webb's analysis has been criticized, perhaps in some respects justly, but this only goes to show how impossible it is to define the characteristics of the West to the satisfaction of everyone.

Texas and Oklahoma are often counted with the South, while large parts of Arkansas and Louisiana have historical affinities with Oklahoma and Texas as western States. Accordingly, I have demarcated two Great Plains States. Greater Missouri, taking up most of the Missouri River basin, would include the Dakotas, Nebraska, Kansas, Montana and Wyoming east of the Continental Divide, eastern Colorado, and a western strip of the present State of Missouri.

Though the Northern Plains States share the Missouri River, its exploitation has been so mishandled—largely because of the rivalry between the Army Engineers and the Bureau of Reclamation—that it is difficult to see how the Missouri Valley States, if they could have acted as one State, could have done a worse job than the Federals. Beginning at the Continental Divide and reading from west to east, the region is notable for mining, cattle and sheep, wheat and corn, and a manufacturing belt, chiefly of industries related to agricultural products. One striking characteristic of the area is that despite its definite feeling of regionalism, its capital is a city outside its borders, Chicago.

The States of the Northern Plains have breadth, height, variety, and character; and they have problems fully as serious as those of any other part of the country. Water-power sites are legion in the Rockies, but either they are not used or the corporations that use them raise the price of electricity to unreasonable heights. The High Plains have been subject to flood and drought, and it was unwise to turn grazing areas into wheat lands. At any rate, overgrazing and dry farming have turned the region into recurrent Dust Bowls. The result is that the Northern Plains States have been the only ones in the nation to decrease in population.

I have suggested the name *Texas* for the Southern Plains, though there may be complaint from Oklahoma and the parts of other States joined to it. It would include Texas (except the El Paso area), Oklahoma, southwestern Missouri, Arkansas west of 92°, and Louisiana west of 92° and north of the 31st parallel, which is a protraction of the northern border of the State's eastern panhandle. Obviously the proposed State includes some mountains—part of the Ozarks, and the eastern slopes of the Rockies, the Sangre de Cristo, and Sacramento Mountains.

The Southern Plains region offers a startling contrast to the Missouri Valley, not only in its superior resources but in the way it has developed. It is true that the area also has its problems of water, corporation domination, and Dust Bowl, and in addition acute minority problems with its Negro and Mexican populations. The difference may lie partly in the greater resources of the Southern Plains and partly in the frontier vigor of its people, but one suspects that it lies even more in the intense local patriotism that rose from Texas' consciousness of its mere *size* and its unique history. If the Missouri Valley had developed as one state, it is possible that it also would have exhibited many of the same characteristics.

The rest of the nation views the "beaming self-satisfaction" of Texans with attitudes that range from amused fondness to affectionate contempt. Texas, they quote, has "more cattle and less milk, more rivers and less water, more schools and less education, more miles of view and less to see than any place on earth." Once at a banquet the Governor of Texas introduced the Governor of Oklahoma, "an outlying state of Texas." The guest rose to the occasion. "I want it understood here and now," he replied, " that *no* state out lies Texas!" However all this may be, the men who give names to books and movies insist that the word *Texas* in the title means money all over the nation. Texas is the epitome of the American manias for bigness and for self-advertisement. It has the most intense localism in the United States—Virginia, Indiana, Missouri, and California pale beside it, and even the narcissism of New York City is clouded. Texans regard themselves as a race apart, and the highest cachet a man can bear is to be a native-born Texan. There is a becoming note of modesty (Texas size) in the saying: "Never ask a man where he comes from. If he's a Texan, he'll tell you; if he's not, don't embarrass him."

In a sense Texas is still in the Jacksonian Era, which was a welter of anti-intellectuals, Bible shouters, populists, political lickspittles, and worshippers of social mediocrity and material accomplishment. Yet it must not be forgotten that the Jacksonian Era held the seeds of all that has made the United States a great material and spiritual power. The eastern area of Texas, rather closely allied to the South, holds most of the cotton fields, the petroleum and gas wells, and the industries based largely on sulphur and petroleum products. The lower wedge of Texas is largely given over to cattle, except that irrigated land on the lower Rio Grande raises vegetables and citrus fruits, including the famous pink-meat Texas grapefruit.

Eastern Oklahoma, the old Indian Territory, holds about a third of the Indians of the United States, but most of them are so nearly assimilated to white civilization that Oklahomans are of all Westerners least conscious of an Indian problem.

Texas, however, has a heavy Negro population in its eastern portion and as heavy a proportion of citizens of Mexican extraction down its central axis and in its west.

What is the regional capital of the Texas-Southwest? Dallas-Forth Worth and Houston, each with about two million people in its metropolitan area, each claims the honor, but neither has proved its claim. In any case, as one of its sons observed, "Texas is today the largest and most profitable colony in the world." Its railways, its petroleum corporations, and its new chemical industries are held in the fists of men in the North.

THE FAR WEST

When we look at the Far West (beyond the backbone of the Rocky and the Sangre de Cristo Mountains), we find that it falls into six principal subregions with jagged boundaries: (1) California west of the Sierra Nevada; (2) Southern California, the area south of the Tehachapi Mountains; (3) the Colorado Valley; (4) the Great Basin, the area between the Sierras and the Colorado Valley; (5) the Rio Grande Valley in New Mexico; and (6) the Columbia Valley. In a sense the Far West is a congeries of subregions rather than a region. There is relatively little communication among many of its parts. For example, though almost all the mountain ranges run north and south, most of the roads and railroads run east and west. State lines were drawn up to suit political exigencies or without much understanding of the climatic and other natural factors involved.

The states of the Far West have in common their colonial subjection to the East and the fact that their water resources are not distributed by Nature at the points where they are most needed. Of course, there is not enough water to irrigate the entire Far West even if that were topographically possible, but there is plenty of water for urban and farm use for a population possibly as great as that of the United States today, should one dare dream of such a thing in this day of ecological alarm. However this may be, we can be sure that vast areas of the Far West will always remain the refuge of solitude. The problem, then, is not so much the scarcity of water as its seasonal and geographical distribution, and not less the baffling technical, chemical, and economic problems that follow on any attempt to use it.

Just as troublesome are the problems of politics and vested interests that are involved and that frequently doom any integrated effort to develop or preserve resources for the future. "What," demand some Westerners, "has posterity done for us?" They resent Eastern exploitation, but frequently the attitude rises less from a desire to preserve and use their heritage wisely than from a desire to share the gravy. Eastern interests never have any difficulty finding allies in any Western state. There are Western lawyers and publicists who for a price will rationalize discrimination in freight rates and high mortgage rates on real estate, who will find reasons for opening the national forests (and even the national parks) to unlimited grazing, timber cutting, and power exploitation.

A third and sometimes no less potent welding factor in the Far West is a common fear and distrust of California. Not only is California the oldest and most mature area, but its population and developed wealth is probably double that of all the rest of the Far West combined. For generations it was separated from the remainder of the nation by a vast, sparsely inhabited area. Endowed with statehood within two years after the gold strike and guided by a group of articulate writers, politicians, and self-sufficient financiers, California came to look on itself as a nation and, like a nation, developed its own regional and economic clashes for power and its own imperial tentacles. An urban State almost from the first, it was harassed by labor and agrarian discontent and dominated by mining, railroad, irrigation, real estate, power, and food-growing and processing corporations.

San Francisco became a branch office of Wall Street, entrusted with the administration of the Far West. It was willing to accept disadvantages vis-à-vis the East in return for superior advantages in intraregional competition. As a result the Far West came to regard California as an exploiter and in many ways a double-dealer. California has managed to divert to its own use water that should go to Nevada and, despite an interstate compact, it has managed to get the lion's share of Colorado River water and power—to the detriment of the Great Basin and Colorado Valley states. The development of the Central Valley has been left pretty much to the Federal government.

San Francisco has had a turbulent economic and political history, but it early began to develop in the usual American urban pattern. More than this, as the undisputed capital of the Far West it took on a sophistication and cosmopolitanism found elsewhere only in New York. It is not without significance that the San Francisco area boasts the most varied and colorful residents, the best restaurants, the most vocal labor movement, and the oldest and—until recently—most respected institution of higher learning on the Pacific Coast. But it also has skeletons in its closet—civic corruption, corporate domination, race violence and, of course, earthquakes. The calamity of 1906, when an earthquake shook down the city and fed it to the flames, is still referred to by loyal 'Ciscans as "The Fire." San Francisco, be it recorded, is the place where a city father issued the famous call to civic betterment: "Let us grab the bull by the tail and look the facts squarely in the face."

TWO CALIFORNIAS

Though fear of California may seem to many Far Westerners a legitimate reason for dividing it, I do not for a moment suppose that San Francisco's economic imperialism would disappear with such an action. My proposal is based on quite different reasons. California falls naturally into several sub-regions, of which the "Bay Area" around San Francisco is only one. There is also the rugged north, with the famous *Sequoia Sempervirens* along the coast and other lumbering and some cattle interests. Then there is the Sierra Nevada Range, with its unexcelled national parks and its summer and winter resorts. The Central Valley of California is the heart of the State, a bowl about 500 miles long and 100 miles wide, which with climate and gigantic irrigation projects has become a natural hothouse for the production of fruits and vegetables.

Each of these sub-regions has its own characteristics and economic interests, and though the Bay Area has burgeoned, it is still logically related to the North, to the Sierras, and to the Central Valley.

Conditions are different in Southern California, which is quite literally cut off from the rest of the state by natural barriers and by the fact that the Central Valley has traditionally looked toward San Francisco, to which it has easy access.

Southern California occupies about a quarter of the State, but by far the most of it is uninhabitable. A strip about 300 miles long from San Luis Obispo southward and never more than about sixty miles wide holds approximately half of California's population and wealth. The metropolitan area of Los Angeles has about 8.5 million, while San Diego, known to the nation chiefly as a Marine Corps and naval base, is a flourishing district of about 1.25 million. In the eyes of most Easterners, Southern California *is* California. It is known for oranges, movie studios, forests of oil derricks, and religious, dietary, economic, and political fads and cults. Probably there is too much leisure and boredom, too much loosening of life-long inhibitions among these "refugees from America." Aldous Huxley satirized Los Angeles as the City of Dreadful Joy—then decided to stay on. Southern California is a huge paradox. Its people are not inclined to go to much trouble, yet they have a mania for getting things done. There is intense materialism and a suspicion of abstract thought, yet the region is host to swarms of artists and intellectuals who are profoundly affecting American culture. Labor is taking over and reading the riot act to industry in an area where a generation ago a man was arrested for attempting to read the Declaration of Independence in public. It is a land of many moods: hospitable to reaction and to change, to sound ideas and to silly panaceas, to eccentricity and to the humdrum virtues.

The city of Los Angeles has grown by explosion. It is unique in the spotty way in which it has swallowed up hunks and patches of territory and has even reached a long tentacle southward to engulf the port of San Pedro, twenty miles from city hall. New suburbs rise, literally in a season, consisting of thousands of homes and complete with schools, churches, theaters, shopping centers, and bus lines. But with all its explosive efficiency, Los Angeles has done little to solve the problem of public transportation, so that it has become the city par excellence of the automobile and the freeway. Los Angeles is a network of suburbs, each generally inhabited by people with similar interests, tasks, or economic standards. But economically Los Angeles and its parts and suburbs cannot be considered apart; along with the *rentier* who depends on investments, the lifeblood of the complex lies in oil wells, movies for video, airplane factories, and numerous small fabricating plants, usually branches of Eastern corporations. Moreover, Los Angeles can boast more Mexicans than any single place outside of Mexico City and Guadalajara, and more Negroes than any other city in the West.

The proposal to divide California into two States is at least as old as this century. The rivalry between north and south has grown with the burgeoning of Los Angeles, but apparently always founders on which end shall keep the name *California.* Presumably North California and South California are not acceptable. Actually, the name was first used by the Spanish for the southern area, adjacent to what is now Mexico's State of Baja California, but it spread northward with the spread of the missions. The Gold Rush of 1849 popularized the Sacramento Valley as California, but before 1900 the Huntingtons and other real estate promoters had made Southern California a synonym for paradise in the American lexicon. I propose to cut the Gordian knot by setting apart the southern part under the name *California;* it would really be a city-state like New York and Chicago, but with the Mojave Desert attached. The north, from the sea to the eastern limits of the Sacramento River Basin and the crest of the Sierra Nevada Mountains and south to the Tehachapi Mountains, could be called *Sierra*— though there are other names available, such as *Sequoia,* from its redwoods, and *Sonoma* and *Monterey,* from its early settlements.

A GREATER OREGON

About the new state of Oregon there can be little cavil, for it is united by the Columbia River. The Columbia Valley includes Washington, Oregon, Idaho, and parts of the neighboring states and Canada; the Puget Sound and Rogue River areas are inseparable sharers of its riches and its problems. West of the Cascade Mountains this subregion differs from the rest of the Far West in that the Japan Current brings it plentiful rain and makes it green and temperate. Here are the great urban districts of Seattle (1.25 million) on Puget Sound, and Portland (1 million) at the mouth of the Williamette ("the Will*am*ette, God damn it!"), some manufacturing, and a great deal of lumbering, fishing, and general farming. Seattle's significance rises not only from its rich hinterland and its advantage as the terminal of three transcontinental railways, but from the fact that it is the entrepot for Alaska's gold, copper, fish, and timber.

East of the Cascades the summers are hot and dry and the winters severe and snowy. Mining, lumbering, wheat growing, and cattle grazing are the pattern in the east, together with some irrigation, which produces such products as the famous Idaho potatoes. The only considerable city in the east is Spokane, which claims the mastery of the upper valley. Idaho is one of the least logically composed of the States. Its three settled areas owe allegiance to Spokane, Salt Lake City, and Oregon, while between them lies an area, as large as Connecticut, that is scarcely removed from primitive solitude.

The great fact about the Columbia River Valley is that in all the Far West it has the most favorable conditions for conquering the perennial problems of water and power and for developing a self-sufficient agricultural and industrial economy. Here the New Deal began to develop the second largest river on the continent. The Army engineers built Bonneville Dam (1939) above Portland, and the Bureau of Reclamation built enormous Grand Coulee Dam (1942). World War II put the newly available power to work in dozens of new enterprises, most notable of them the atomic energy plant at Hanford. Swarms of people moved in, chiefly from the Missouri Valley, and stayed when the war was over.

The situation cries for an integrated plan of administration and utilization of resources—a Columbia Valley Authority—yet the usual conservative forces have managed to stave it off. The fact is that Northwesterners are suspicious of too many changes of any kind. There is too much rain in the west, but the country is green; the cities lack many of the cultural features enjoyed in other places, but they are manageable in size, and it is possible to escape for a weekend without being crushed in traffic—or it was until recently. There is a sense of relaxation and of plenty of time to spend, a feeling of permanence and assurance. The simple fact is that the citizens of the Columbia Valley live in one of the pleasantest regions in the world, and they know it and want it to remain that way.

DESERET

The interior country south of the new Oregon and from the crest of the Sierra Nevada to the Continental Divide and the Sangre de Cristo Mountains I propose to unite under the name *Deseret,* from Brigham Young's dream of the "Land of the Honey Bee." The Colorado River Valley States have benefited greatly by the Hoover Dam, but they have not had the money to construct the elaborate public works that they envisioned and that presumably would have made the desert blossom like the rose. Arizona has about 1.7 million people, and these are mostly congregated about the mining towns and the irrigated areas, of which Phoenix and Tucson are the centers.

The Great Basin includes most of Nevada and parts of Utah, Idaho, Oregon, and California. Unlike other parts of the United States, it has no considerable rivers, and those smaller streams it does have vanish into salt lakes or into the sand. Nevada, with less than 500,000 people, lives on sheep, cattle, mining, gambling percentages, and the board-money attracted by a divorce mill. Dependent for water and power on California's Sierras and with its financial capital in San Francisco, it has had no choice but to play second fiddle to its great neighbor. Utah is better off, with a million people, most of whom are vigorous, thrifty, hard-working Mormons. Too, the economic power of Utah is largely in the hands of the Mormon Church, one of the most successful cooperative enterprises in history. The population of Utah is centered largely in the agricultural north, along the Logan-Ogden-Salt Lake City-Provo axis, but continues diagonally southwest in a narrow strip along the old "Mormon Corridor."

The upper valley of the Rio Grande should be a part of Deseret. New Mexico is the seat of an old and dignified Indian-Spanish-Catholic culture based on sheep, cattle, and irrigated land that grows respectable quantities of cotton. But over-grazing on the uplands has loosened the soil and is pouring mud into the valleys and dams along the Rio Grande, with the prospect that the entire irrigation system will soon be ruined. It is significant that El Paso is the queen of southern New Mexico and Amarillo of the northeast. Neither bustling Albuquerque nor the scenic capital city of Santa Fe can hope to compete with them. But then El Paso, at least, should also be in Deseret. Just how far Deseret's mining and industry can be developed remains to be seen, for its resources have never been fully mapped.

THE PROPOSED STATES AND THE THREAT OF IMPERIALISM

It may have occurred to the reader that the organization of regions as States on topographic, climatic, historical, and cultural lines might well result in the creation of nascent nations. I have been well aware of this: indeed, Frederick Jackson Turner anticipated that as the States of each of the sections drew together in defense of their common interests, the character of our federalism would be greatly altered.

> As the nation reaches a more stable equilibrium, a more settled state of society, with denser populations pressing upon the means of existence, with this popula-tion no longer migratory, the influence of the diverse physiographic provinces which make up the nation will become more marked. They will exercise section-alizing influences, tending to mould society to their separate conditions, in spite of all the countervailing tendencies toward national uniformity. National action will be forced to recognize and adjust itself to these conflicting sectional interests. The more the nation is organized on the principle of direct majority rule, and consolidation, the more sectional resistance is likely to manifest itself. Statesmen in the future, as in the past, will achieve their leadership by voicing the interests and ideas of the sections which have shaped these leaders, and they will exert their influence nationally by making combinations between sections and by accommodating their policy to the needs of such alliances. Congressional legisla-tion will be shaped by compromises and combinations, which will in effect be treaties between rival sections, and the real federal aspect of our government will lie, not in the relation of state and nation, but in the relation of section and nation.[4]

---

[4] *The Significance of Sections in American History* (New York: Holt, 1932), pages 313-314. Reprinted by permission.

The problem, of course, is how to preserve America's precious pluralism without encouraging regional insularity. Turner made no serious attempt to forecast just what would happen, but enough markers have appeared in the last half-century to enable one to warn that unless a new form of federalism is worked out, we are likely, when a real disaster strikes, to disintegrate or turn to a Caesar for salvation.

Thus far I have not mentioned the possibility that a new State or alliance of States might assume imperial control of the country. This has been much the situation since the Civil War, for the Northeast—especially New York City—has pretty well dictated national policies, using Chicago and San Francisco as branch offices. The New Deal's emphasis on regional development began to loosen New York's control, and the movement is still under way. Nevertheless, I am fully aware of the danger of imperialism, and much of the remainder of this book will be devoted to proposing ways to block it.

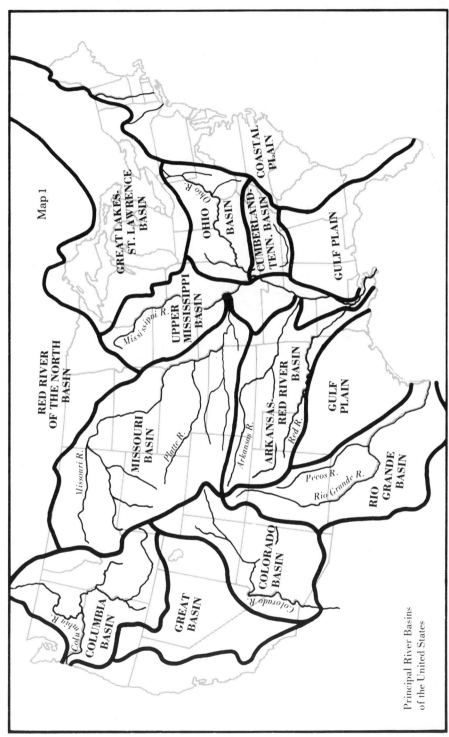

Map 1

GREAT LAKES-
ST. LAWRENCE
BASIN

OHIO
BASIN

Ohio R.

CUMBERLAND-
TENN. BASIN

COASTAL
PLAIN

GULF PLAIN

RED RIVER
OF THE NORTH
BASIN

UPPER
MISSISSIPPI
BASIN

Mississippi R.

MISSOURI
BASIN

Missouri R.

Platte R.

Arkansas R.

ARKANSAS-
RED RIVER
BASIN

Red R.

GULF
PLAIN

Pecos R.

Rio Grande R.

RIO
GRANDE
BASIN

COLUMBIA
BASIN

Columbia R.

GREAT
BASIN

COLORADO
BASIN

Colorado R.

Principal River Basins
of the United States

57

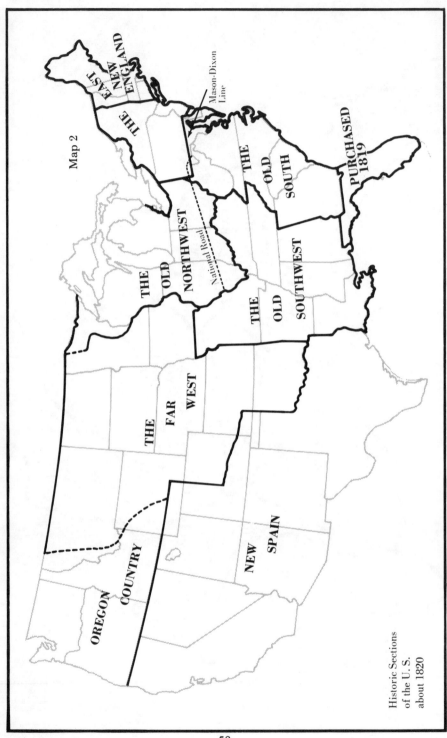

Map 2

EAST NEW ENGLAND

THE

Mason-Dixon Line

THE OLD SOUTH

PURCHASED 1819

THE OLD NORTHWEST

National Road

THE OLD SOUTHWEST

THE FAR WEST

OREGON COUNTRY

NEW SPAIN

Historic Sections
of the U. S.
about 1820

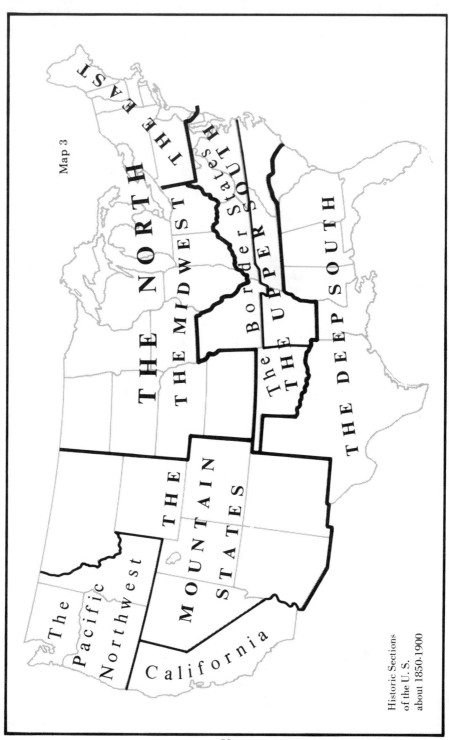

Map 3

THE NORTH

THE EAST

THE MIDWEST

Border State?

THE UPPER SOUTH

The

THE DEEP SOUTH

THE MOUNTAIN STATES

The Pacific Northwest

California

Historic Sections
of the U. S.
about 1850-1900

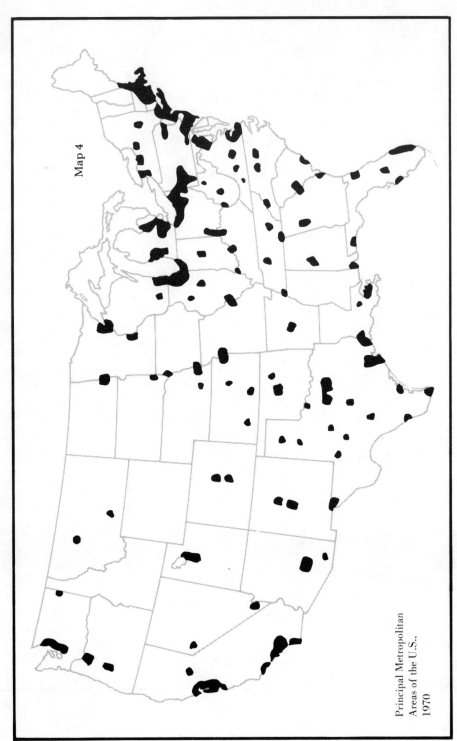

Map 4

Principal Metropolitan
Areas of the U.S.
1970

60

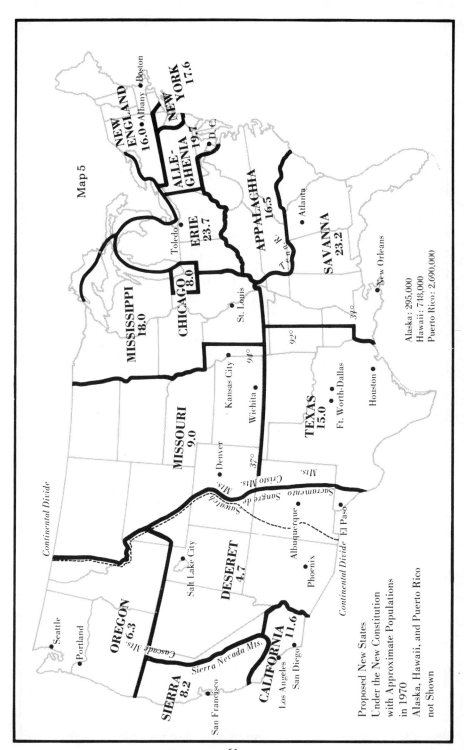

Map 5

NEW ENGLAND 16.0 • Albany • Boston
NEW YORK 17.6
ALLE-GHENIA 19.7 • D.C.
APPALACHIA 16.5
ERIE 23.7 • Toledo
SAVANNA 23.2 • Atlanta
CHICAGO 18.0
• New Orleans
MISSISSIPPI 18.0
• St. Louis
37°
Kansas City
• Wichita 94° 92°
MISSOURI 9.0
• Denver
TEXAS 15.0
• Ft. Worth-Dallas
Houston •
Sangre de Cristo Mts. Mts. 37°
Sacramento Mts.
• Albuquerque
El Paso • Continental Divide
Continental Divide
DESERET 4.7
• Salt Lake City
• Phoenix
OREGON 6.3
• Seattle
• Portland
Cascade Mts.
SIERRA 8.2
Sierra Nevada Mts.
• San Francisco
CALIFORNIA 11.6
• Los Angeles
• San Diego

Alaska: 295,000
Hawaii: 718,000
Puerto Rico: 2,690,000

Proposed New States
Under the New Constitution
with Approximate Populations
in 1970
Alaska, Hawaii, and Puerto Rico
not Shown

61

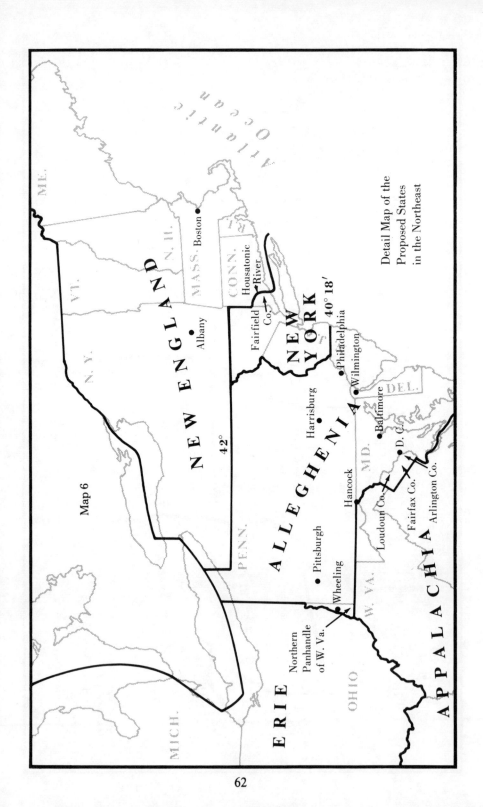

Map 6

Detail Map of the
Proposed States
in the Northeast

NEW ENGLAND

NEW YORK

ALLEGHENIA

ERIE

APPALACHIA

MICH.

ME.

N.H.

VT.

N.Y.

MASS.

CONN.

Boston

Atlantic Ocean

Housatonic
River

Fairfield
Co.

Albany

42°

40° 18′

Philadelphia

Wilmington

DEL.

Baltimore

MD.

Harrisburg

D. C.

PENN.

Hancock

Loudoun Co.

Fairfax Co.

Arlington Co.

Pittsburgh

Wheeling

W. VA.

Northern
Panhandle
of W. Va.

OHIO

62

Chapter 5

THE SEPARATION OF POWERS

THE IRRESISTIBLE PRESIDENT AND THE IMMOVABLE CONGRESS

When we come to separation of powers, we enter a thicket—or rather a cluster of thickets—through which it is not certain we can ever find our way. These thickets are the lairs of at least four hoary institutions, no less powerful, at least in their obstructive abilities, than the courthouse gangs, the States, and the Federal bureaucracy. They are, of course, the President, the Senate, the House of Representatives, and the Supreme Court. For a century, and from time to time, each of them has claimed the right to interpret the Constitution. Even now each of them devotes much of its time to obstructing the others while it labors to surmount the obstructions they have strewn in its path. Here we shall be concerned chiefly with the President and Congress.

The President, as the only responsible official elected by all the people—even though not directly—is the person most likely to see problems in their national and international context, but he is continually being obstructed by Senators and Representatives. That is because the lawmaker is primarily concerned with two things: (1) a constituency in which the most active elements are business interests with axes to grind and voters who judge him by the pork he brings home; and (2) getting reelected so that he will acquire the seniority essential to building a power base in Congress. Personal antipathies may also play a part. It seems clear that the antipathy between Woodrow Wilson and Henry Cabot Lodge was one reason for the Senate's rejection of the League of Nations. There are other instances that apparently shifted the course of American history—for example, the antipathy between John Marshall and Thomas Jefferson and between John Calhoun and Andrew Jackson.

The result, inevitably, is that the President—frequently denounced by critics as irresistible—collides with an immovable Congress. Even when Congress yields, it sometimes sews so many hooks into the legal fabric that the President finds himself immobilized. It is not necessary to probe very far for an example. President Kennedy made a brave start, but at the time of his assassination was essentially stymied by Congress. President Johnson managed to push through what was essentially the Kennedy program, partly by cashing in the I.O.U.'s he had collected as a Congressional leader, partly because Congress had a guilty conscience about blocking Kennedy, and partly because in 1964 the Republican Party seriously misjudged the temper of the country, with the result that over forty liberal Representatives were swept into the House. The bogging down of the Great Society program was by no means due solely to the Vietnam War; the liberal Representatives were defeated in 1966, Johnson had run out of I.O.U.'s, and the ghost of John Kennedy had been exorcised, so that Congress could resume its obstructionism.

It is all very well to attribute the foregoing situations to the greed and rivalries of ambitious and power-hungry men, but the cause runs deeper. It lies also in the nature of the Constitution, which (1) inevitably makes antagonists of President and Congress, and (2) permits the States to mark out the Congressional districts, say who can vote, and set the terms of the local party organization to which Congressmen are obligated.

Actually, the confusion and hard-headedness of Congress is nothing new, but has existed from the beginning. James S. Young, in *The Washington Community: 1800–1828* (1966), graphically describes the rivalries among the branches of government in the early years of the republic, and shows how they effectively paralyzed most action. Moreover, Congress itself was so divided among partisans and sections that a British visitor could call it "a deliberative body come to discuss a question in a spirit of avowed misunderstanding, without the smallest wish to agree." There was a pioneer saying that "a man has to do what he has to do" —that is, make up his mind, right or wrong, and then go ahead. Congress has never learned this lesson, but all too often does little more than vacillate or throw obstacles in the way of effective administration.

Time and custom have contrived to conceal political spitefulness from the public with a veneer of punctilio, but Washingtonians are well aware of what still lies just beneath the surface. The situation is so bad that President, Senate, and House sometimes block each other just to be mean. Thus Senate or House may adopt a popular measure of which it disapproves, knowing full well that the other House must strike it down or the President veto it.

Reprinted by permission of Newspaper Enterprise
Association, Inc.

By no means all the obstacles to rational and effective government are written
into the Constitution; many of them have come about by extension or by custom.
The President's power over the military has been used to wage undeclared war
all through American history—one estimate puts it at 149 times—beginning with
the Barbary Wars, and it has only recently been seriously questioned by Congress.
The President has also made hundreds of "agreements" with foreign powers
without consulting the Senate, on matters ranging from hunting migratory birds
and growing opium poppies to leasing military bases in Spain.

Our system of separation of powers can work only so long as competing
politicians are able to form a web of alliances that gives an illusion of stability.
But such a structure is certain to collapse when a vitally divisive issue arises. The
controversy over extending slavery to the territories provided such an issue, and
gave rise to clashing Constitutional interpretations, and finally to civil war. For
a generation after Reconstruction, politicians preferred to deal with superficiali-
ties, for they feared that any attempt to deal with the cankers eating at the vitals
of the nation would cause another civil war. However that may have been, House
partisans so consistently blocked legislation that Republican Speakers assumed
autocratic powers over committee appointments and the introduction of bills. In
1910 the House revolted and sheared the Speaker of his power to decide what
legislation could be called up and when. This opened the way for the chairmen
of committees to become czars able to refuse to allow a bill to be considered, or

even to refuse to call their committees together. Since chairmen were customarily the senior members of the majority party, the way was thus open for rule by senility. The Speakership also devolved upon a senior Representative, often regardless of his fitness.

Reprinted by permission of The King Features Syndicate.

Normally, then, the House is controlled by men who are slaves to outmoded ideas and customs. Government by senility in the House is matched in the Senate but is sometimes made even worse by the "Senatorial courtesy" which enables a Senator—at least one in the majority party—to veto a Presidential appointment in his State, perhaps even to dictate who shall be appointed. Thus, when a Senator or Representative has gone to Washington, he has been confined to the Iron Virgin of the seniority system from which there is no escape unless he can build his own empire. Recent moves to temper the seniority system may or may not be fake passes.[1]

THE FOUR-PARTY SYSTEM

By now it should be clear that one of the problems which always comes to the fore in discussing a change in our President-Congress form of government is this: will the President dominate Congress or will Congress dominate the President?

---

[1]Good references on President and Congress are Douglass Cater, *Power in Washington* (New York: Random House, 1964); Richard E. Neustadt, *Presidential Power* (New York: Wiley, 1960); and George E. Reedy, *The Twilight of the Presidency* (New York: World, 1970).

There is no certain answer, for a great deal depends on the qualities of each. Under the present system every President is faced with the thorny problem of how he can work with the Congressional leaders even of his own party. Congressmen, of course, can be honestly uncertain of where their duty lies. Is their first obligation to their House, or is it to promote the President's program?

Much light has been thrown on these problems by the recent researches of political scientists. Some of them have lately taken to speaking of our politics as being organized not as a two-party system but as a four-party system. James MacGregor Burns finds the origin of this condition in the clashing concepts of Madison and Jefferson, the former favoring Congressional supremacy in forming policies, the latter favoring Presidential initiative. Though the theory has been challenged, it is persuasive enough to deserve presentation. To cut the long historical story short, the United States, says Burns, has operated under both the Madisonian system of checks and balances and the Jeffersonian system of majority and Presidential rule, with the result that, save in the most vital national crises, the political troops are riding off in all directions. Both Democrats and Republicans are divided into Congressional and Presidential factions. In the ordinary course of legislative business, the Congressional factions of the two parties are more likely to cooperate with each other than either is to cooperate with the Presidential faction of its own party.

During the 1830's the Whigs became so bitterly critical of Jackson that they adopted the Madisonian view and sought to strip the Presidency of all but the most limited executive powers, an attitude that became known as the Whig concept of the Presidency. This concept has been most prevalent among Southern Democrats and Republicans from rural constituencies, and it is notable that there have been only two strong Republican Presidents—Lincoln and Theodore Roosevelt. Moreover, historically, the Republican Party seldom has nominated Presidential candidates who gave promise of executive strength; only Willkie and Dewey come to mind, though of course, many other nominees were estimable men. It should be noted, too, that Lincoln owed his nomination at least partly to the opinion of the party bosses that he would be malleable, while Theodore Roosevelt became President by accident.

The Democratic Party has been less reluctant to put up strong candidates— and this despite the two-thirds rule which until 1936 gave the South a veto on the nomination in the national convention. We can point to Cleveland, Wilson, Franklin Roosevelt, and Kennedy, who won, and to Tilden, Smith, Stevenson, and Humphrey, who lost, and to the accidental Presidents, Truman and Lyndon Johnson. (There have been exceptions, notably Bryan, Parker, and Davis.)

Regardless of party tendencies, Burns maintains that the Congressional factions in both parties normally rule the Federal bureaucracy, insofar as it can be ruled at all. True, Congressional committee chairmen will sometimes be helpful to bureaucrats if the latter are subservient enough—as the Pentagon is to the armed services committees. But the Congressional parties control the Congressional machinery lock, stock, and barrel, regardless of who is President. "Senatorial courtesy" limits Presidential appointments to office in the States, and the Senate has a veto on many other appointments—and uses it. Congress can financially starve an unpopular bureau or agency, and its investigating committees can —and do—harass bureaucrats until they resign or take refuge in a hospital. In contrast to the almost continual rapport between the Congressional factions, there is almost no way in which the Presidential parties can cooperate.

In its campaign to limit executive power, Congress has resorted to a device used by the colonial assemblies to hamstring their governors—the appointment of commissions. The Constitution does not permit the same agency to exercise executive, legislative, and judicial powers, and so Congress has set up "quasi-judicial" commissions to exercise the powers it fears to give the President—over such things as interstate commerce, water power, the stock market, and interstate industrial competition. The courts have obligingly declared that such an administrative agency merely "seems to be" exercising judicial or legislative power.

The reasons given for setting up this form of regulatory commission were to protect them from political interference and enable them to concentrate on a function new to the Federal government—regulation of the economy. Nevertheless, a number of legislators and political scientists are sure that the "headless fourth branch" was intended basically to avoid increasing executive power. It is difficult to avoid the impression, too, that in many cases it was the intention of Congress to thwart impartial administration, for these regulatory agencies have quite often taken on a life of their own independent of both President and Congress and have become subservient to the very interests on which they are supposed to ride herd. As Burns observes, these agencies are by no means "out of politics" but have become more or less willing tools of special interests.

The Bourbon-Old Guard alliance between the Congressional Southern Democrats and the conservative Northern Republicans has been a fact of politics for almost a century. Only when a strong President and a surge of popular emotion happen to coincide, as they did under the New Freedom, the New Deal, and the Great Society—only then can significant social and economic reform be forced down the throats of the Bourbon-Old Guard coalition. And it is notable that in all three cases the promises of reform were cut short by war.

HOW DOES THE PRESIDENTIAL FACTION SURVIVE?

Some political scientists have objected to Burns's four-party division, but if we accept it there must be some wonderment that the Presidential parties have managed to survive. One reason is that Congressional leaders have sometimes misjudged their candidate, as they certainly did in the case of Lincoln and may have in the case of Franklin Roosevelt. Another reason, of course, is that accidental Presidents sometimes prove to be stronger than expected—witness Theodore Roosevelt, Harry Truman, and Lyndon Johnson.

"Sure good to be back in harness again." (Fischetti, NEA)

Reprinted by permission of the Newspaper Enterprise Association, Inc.

Burns attributes the survival of the Presidential parties chiefly, however, to the quadrennial national Presidential nominating convention. The convention originated in the 1830's as an alternative to the nomination of candidates by caucuses of Congressional partisans. In retrospect, it would seem that the caucus method was a good one, but disappointed aspirants called it King Caucus and whipped up popular resistance to it. Congressmen have invariably been prominent in conventions, but they have rarely been able to override the desires of an incumbent President, nor have they always managed to withstand the desires of delegates, who come much closer to representing the rank-and-file of the party than do Congressmen. Frequently Congressmen yield to the demands of the delegates on the ground that the popular choice is more "electable" than the man they prefer. Thus Wilson triumphed over Champ Clark, Franklin Roosevelt over Jack Garner, Dewey and Eisenhower over Robert Taft, Stevenson over Barkley and Kefauver, and Kennedy over Johnson. Even so, the Congressional faction normally writes the party platform and nominates a Congressional favorite for the Vice-Presidency.

Another strength of the Presidential faction is that the voters regard a Presidential election as more significant than an "off-year" election, and so flock to the polls in greater numbers in Presidential years. Thus it is possible for a popular candidate to carry in a sympathetic Congress "on his coattails," as Franklin Roosevelt did in 1932 and 1936, and Lyndon Johnson did in 1964—but as Eisenhower did not do in 1956, nor Nixon in 1968. National issues normally receive more attention in Presidential years, and suppliants for Federal largesse are more likely to be aware that their interests are at stake. "Off-year" elections usually hinge on local interests and pressures, and the Congressional factions are likely to recoup whatever losses they suffered two years before. In any case, Congressional leaders usually come from "safe" districts, which return them year after year and enable them to amass the seniority that is the key to power in Congress.

Ordinarily a strong President can control the party machinery—that is, outside of Congress—and even a weak President can be almost certain of renomination. On the other hand, a defeated Presidential candidate has no control over the party machinery, and it falls into the control of the Congressional faction until the next convention revives the Presidential faction. Nor can a President be assured that his appointments to the Supreme Court will follow his program or strengthen his faction, for a President may misjudge his appointees. Theodore Roosevelt colorfully expressed his disappointment with Holmes, and Eisenhower found Earl Warren blandly undermining the President's "moderate progressivism"—or was it "moderate conservatism"?

The exception that proves the rule was John Adams' appointment of John Marshall as Chief Justice, for Marshall by sheer personality and genius in group persuasion was able to make the Court a Federalist bastion regardless of what Justices were appointed by opposition Presidents. Franklin Roosevelt's appointees did accept his basic doctrine that Federal power should be expanded, but split apart on methods. The impartial historian must judge the cost to the nation of the Court's assumption of powers the Framers never intended it to possess. Marshall knew he was performing unconstitutionally, as is proved by his agony of spirit before he wrote the decision in the case of *Marbury v. Madison.* I shall return to the Supreme Court in a later chapter.

Of course, one cannot draw a neat ideological line between the Congressional factions on one side and the Presidential factions on the other. Nor can one say that all Congressmen oppose the President, for there always are Senators and Representatives who oppose the Whig concept of the Presidency. Moreover, party ties frequently influence Congressional leaders to support a President of their party. And then, of course, the President is often supported by the corps of administrative and judicial officers (district attorneys and marshals) whom he has appointed.

Generally the Presidential party is made up of Northern Democrats or Northern Establishment Republicans. In either case it is likely to be the popular party, the one favored by the voters, and one that is eager to expand Federal powers and do all it can to see that the people get a square deal. It can afford these attitudes because it is not under the same intense pressure by local interests as Congressmen. There is, however, this factor to be considered: the split between those who worship the Constitution as an obstacle to effective government (that is, to change) and those who have come to look on the President as the protector of civil rights for minority groups—blacks, Chicanos, senior citizens, and others.[2]

A discouraging fact of the present legislative problem lies in the difficulty of orienting the Representative toward national problems—to break his obligation to the local machine. Until some way is found of handling most less-than-national affairs by some agency, such as the region, that is large enough to be viable and so to assume control of most local concerns, Congress will be over-burdened—and over-powerful. At present, Congressmen deal not only with national and international affairs but with numerous appropriations and regulations affecting localities. This means that in order to survive they must heed the voices back in the brush country; and this is still true regardless of the power bases they build on Capitol Hill. Surely practical politicians and political scientists can find an answer.

THE BICAMERAL SYSTEM

Let us turn now to the bicameral legislative system. It is said that when Jefferson first returned from Paris to become Secretary of State, he was asked to tea by President Washington. Finding his tea too hot to drink, Jefferson poured some of it into his saucer—which was perfectly proper in those days. Presently Jefferson asked Washington why the Constitutional Convention had provided for two legislative bodies.

"Why did you pour your tea into your saucer?" replied Washington.

"To cool it."

"Exactly," returned the President, "and so will cooler thoughts prevail when legislation passes through two houses."

This anecdote has long been the clincher in rebutting those who criticize the bicameral system—and in the minds of eighteenth century conservatives, it was a reasonable answer. It still is, if one believes—and many people do—that a prime purpose of the Constitution should be to hamper rather than facilitate legislation.

[2]On the four-party system see especially James MacGregor Burns, *The Deadlock of Democracy: Four-Party Politics in America* (Englewood Cliffs, N.J.: Prentice-Hall, 1963), who wrote the most extensive and most persuasive treatment among the several available. It should be noted that he published his book in 1963, and so probably wrote before Kennedy and Johnson revived the Jeffersonian principle of Presidential leadership. For arguments against his thesis see Frank Sorauf, *Political Parties in the American System* (Boston: Little, Brown, 1964), especially Chapter VII, in which the author denies the unity of the Congressional parties. A shrewd analysis of why voters vote as they do is Samuel Lubell, *The Hidden Crisis in American Politics* (New York: Norton, 1970).

As it is, House and Senate have become jealous rivals, cooperating best in obstructing legislation. The cooling process has given way to legislative murder. The
House or Senate mountain labors for months and finally brings forth a legislative
mouse—good or bad—only to have the other House murder it.

We have again and again the tiresome spectacle of each House engaging in
elaborate and repetitive studies and investigations of the conditions with which
proposed legislation is to deal. Unfortunately, these investigations seldom bring
out facts not already known, and it is difficult to escape the conclusion that in
many, many cases they have deteriorated into excuses for putting off decisions
or—worse yet—have become mere vehicles for publicizing the committee chairmen. Since Congressional committees have no power to remove bureaucrats
without an elaborate process of impeachment and trial, it is common practice for
a legislative investigator to go on a "fishing expedition" in search of unpleasant
facts that can be used to force a bureaucrat to become subservient or to resign.
Thus far there seems to be no cure for this, since legislators are notably tolerant
(at least in effect) of one another's peccadillos. Of course, some investigations have
admittedly beneficial results, but can they compensate for the abusive and charac-
ter-destroying actions of a Joe McCarthy and others, many of them still active?
A not uncommon investigator's attitude was expressed by Rep. J. Parnell Thomas
in 1948 to a witness: "The rights you have are the rights given you by this
committee. We will determine what rights you have and what rights you have not
got before the committee."[3]

The true character of Congress, as it now exists, has never been more poignantly expressed than by a man who, as assistant to a senior Senator, was in a
position to know whereof he spoke.

> I have attended many final sessions of the Senate waiting for the magic mo-
> ment of adjournment *sine die*. Senator after Senator rises, and, in the unreal
> insulation that envelops that body, looks back on what was really just another
> year of broken promises, unmet emergencies, sabotaged agendas, farcical investi-
> gations, and fiscal shortages, and hails that year as a triumph of bipartisan
> statesmanship, saluting his colleagues as worthy successors to the Founding
> Fathers. . . . The Congress is the conspicuous failure of the Federal system; that's
> what ought to be said. The Congress is foundering in a virtual morass of incom-
> petence, of pettiness, of parochialism, of moral obtuseness, of procedural and
> institutional atrophy. Arm in arm with the thousand lobbyists who pay the
> campaign bills, Congress has presided over the pollution of our streams, the
> putrefaction of our air, the collapse of our cities, the anarchy of our transporta-

---

[3]On Congressional investigations see Alan Barth, *Government by Investigation* (New York:
Viking, 1955); Rowland Evans, "Louisiana's Passman: The Scourge of Foreign Aid," in
Harper's Magazine, Jan. 1962; and Telford Taylor, *Grand Inquest* (New York: Simon &
Schuster, 1955).

tion system, the cannibalization of our labor relations, the enragement of our minorities, the watering of our currency, the theft of our natural resources. Its heralded achievements are invariably the result of straight-arming by the President or end runs by the Supreme Court. Its failures are peculiarly its own.[4]

Reprinted by permission of The King Features Syndicate.

Now of course the process of shaping legislation does require study and investigation. The problem is to prevent the abuses, which have become more evident than the benefits—at least to the newspaper-reading public. One can reasonably assume that the technique of investigations would be radically altered if the investigators could not reap political profit from them. In the British Parliament the preparation of most legislation devolves upon the appropriate Cabinet member, his parliamentary secretary and committee, and his civil service staff. Investigations of charges of corruption, of the miscarriage of justice, and of delicate problems that need legislative action are often referred to ad hoc Royal Commissions appointed by the Prime Minister (presumably with competent advice) and composed of prominent and knowledgeable citizens and public servants. Investigations are carried out with a minimum of fanfare, and recommendations are usually heeded by the House of Commons. This is quite unlike the attitude of Congress toward the results of many of its own investigations and of Presidential study commissions; one estimate gives the incredible figure of 3,000 commissions working—perhaps "existing" would be a more accurate word—at the Federal level alone.

That there was a degree of wisdom in the system of checks and balances cannot be denied. We need only cite the way in which our attempt to solve modern

---

[4]James Boyd, in *The Washingtonian Magazine,* January 1969, page 55.

problems by increasing the power of the President has not only failed to solve the problems but actually resulted in greater inefficiency and plunged us into foreign ventures of questionable usefulness. But unquestionably the system has helped promote a certain obstructionism among Congressmen, and made them more amenable to outmoded constituent interests and sometimes ready to thwart progress for the pure hell of it.

The above discussion is intended not to argue that we should dispense completely with the division or separation of powers, or with checks and balances, but to show that we should seek to make them more flexible and constructive. A little confusion now and then may be salutary, as indicating that some flexibility and certain choices are still possible; moreover, it ought to make people sit up and think. But we do not need to manufacture confusion; there will always be enough to fill the need.

BLOCKING THE POPULAR WILL

Despite the gloomy motto, "Either Caesar or Nothing," that opens this book, it is not necessary to conclude that we will inevitably be forced to adopt a pseudo-fascist government. When things go wrong the electorate does show a deplorable tendency to blame Washington—especially the President—but that is no proof that the voters are fools. Rather, it seems to me to be an excellent reason for giving Congress and the President more flexibility in making decisions and promoting change, and at the same time making provisions for expertise and for Constitutional guardians; moreover the voter should have more power to force Congress and the President to take notice of the popular will. In brief, this two-fold aim is the thesis of this book. Indeed, I hold that our institutional inflexibility, obstructionism, and diffusion of responsibility have brought us to the present crisis, just as they contributed to the crisis of 1861.

The great majority of the electorate inhabit the middle ground—political, economic and social. This fundamental truism is obscured by a number of conditions, most of them previously noted, which can be summarized here. First, of course, is the inflexibility of the Constitution in the present context—the way in which it slows down change and pits the various parts of government against one another. Second, the internal organization of Congress, especially its hospitality to lobbyists bearing campaign contributions, the seniority system, Senate filibusters, and the long drawn-out and repetitive committee hearings—all these unconscionably delay the implementation of the popular will. Third, the Supreme Court's "Nine Old Men" hold on to life and office long after they have been outmoded by the election returns. Fourth, the President has essentially lost control of the Federal bureaucracy, partly because it is so unwieldy and badly organized, and partly because Congressmen are perpetually interfering. The result is that the President has had to set up policy-study groups in his own office instead of relying on legislators and civil servants who have spent their lives studying alternatives.

Finally, private institutions—corporations, associations, foundations, the news media—are all too often supporters of one extreme or the other, or at least stress them in ways that give false impressions of the relative power of the extremes. Now it is a truism of political science that few of us are wholly liberal or wholly conservative—whatever those terms mean. Rather, we draw some of our opinions from one side and some from the other, and when we cast our votes we are in effect selecting the men and policies that come closest to meeting our wishes. This means that we usually vote for the center, or for something as close to it as we can come. Whenever an extreme draws an unusual number of votes, it is likely to be because of some local or sectional phenomenon, such as the Dixiecrat vote of 1948 and the Wallace vote of 1968; the great exception was the national phenomenon of Barry Goldwater in 1964.

A second truism is that the center moves, perhaps not continuously but at least by perceptible jerks. The last generation has seen a number of liberal—even allegedly radical—proposals adopted. Among them are stock market controls, insurance of bank deposits, union recognition, unemployment insurance, social security, medicare, and Federal aid to the States for use in promoting agriculture, building highways, and financing schools. There has also been a desegregation of public facilities and education, a new emphasis on urban renewal and civil rights, and an extension of the franchise to eighteen-year olds. Obviously not all the details have been worked out, but the backbone of conservative opposition has been broken, and these matters are no longer subjects of political controversy *in principle* among the great majority of voters.

The struggle has passed on to such things as crime, the drug cult, pollution, pornography, abortion, women's liberation, inflation, and school busing. Save among a considerable number of hardheads—and hardhats—even racism is on the way out, for polls show that an ever increasing number of white Americans want the minorities to enjoy the "good things" and the privileges hitherto denied them. True, even though the *principle* is accepted, the details of how and when are more controversial than with those matters named in the preceding paragraph. But the point is that these issues have already reached the center of the political spectrum and so presumably will be satisfactorily settled.[5]

It seems reasonable to conclude that, provided we adapt our institutions wisely, the center will continue to prevail during the near future. But in closing, we

---

[5]Richard M. Scammon and Ben J. Wattenberg, in *The Real Majority* (New York: Coward-McCann, 1970), have brilliantly explored right, left, and center, and emerged with the conclusion that political power in the 1970's will go to the party that most convincingly plants itself in the center. Of course, this does not rule out the aberrant effect that might be exercised by defeat in Vietnam or a stepped-up menace by the communist world. In later chapters I will deal, at least briefly, with some current problems, such as over-population, pollution, and the Faustian drive to over-production, obsolescence, and waste.

should mention another matter, one that will become increasingly significant as computerization is perfected. It requires no particular gift of prescience to foresee that by the end of this century the decisions made by computer will essentially comprise another and presumably impersonal house of legislation in both Federal and State governments, as well as performing much of the bureaucratic labor. The prospect is both hopeful and frightening. Already computerization has been extensively applied in the Bureau of the Budget and the Defense Department, and is getting footholds elsewhere. Indeed, the process may well make the welfare state not only possible but inevitable. Congress is already looking into the possibilities of its general application in collecting and storing data and making decisions.[6]

It is quite possible that computerization will help reduce the present conflict between President and Congress by confronting them with irrefutable data. But it is hard to believe that politics can ever fully become a science; there will always remain some of those characteristics which have led some people to call it an art.

---

[6]The subject is too long and abstruse for extended treatment here, but see John S. Saloma, *Congress and the New Politics* (Boston: Little, Brown, 1969), pages 199-254.

Chapter 6

ON RENOVATING THE PARTY SYSTEM

THE DECLINE OF PARTY RESPONSIBILITY

This chapter will be devoted to the problem of renovating political parties and devising some system of assuring that they perform responsible and responsive roles, but in doing this it will be necessary to deal with the electorate and many of the institutions and functions of government. Still, the fundamental emphasis will be on parties, for their decline is in considerable part responsible for many of the constitutional problems that now make public policy inflexible, throw an unreasonable—even dangerous—share of power and decision making on the President, and give corporate interests and courthouse gangs the opportunity to thrust their ignorance, prejudice, and selfishness into the decision-making processes.

There are a number of reasons for the decline of party responsibility. Television puts emphasis on the personality of the man, not on his party regularity or fertility of ideas. The booming costs of campaigning make it difficult for a young man to get a start in politics; all one has to do to realize this is to look over the roster of candidates for the Senate and for State governorships—not to mention a number of recent Presidential candidates—and note how many of them have personal fortunes or "fat cat" backers. There are a number of books and many articles on campaign financing[1] that the interested reader can consult, and we need give only a few highlights here.

The data on campaign financing is very difficult to estimate because there are many ingenious ways to spend money on behalf of a candidate without reporting it even to him—perhaps especially not to him. Moreover, there is a great deal of free service given by volunteers, donations of cars and planes, printing paper and services, sale of buttons and bumper stickers, dinners, "no-host" cocktail parties to meet the candidate, and expenditures by office holders, businessmen, industries, medical associations, and labor unions. Among reported items small contributions add up, but even more significant is the organization of $1000 clubs, whose members will be invited to a reception at the White House if their candidate wins; dinner at the White House and a political or diplomatic office may cost $10,000. At any rate, hash has been made of the laws professing to govern campaign expenditures.

The money is spent in innumerable ways. To begin with, it may cost millions merely to get a chance at a Presidential nomination; Nelson Rockefeller is said to have spent $5 million in 1964 in his unsuccessful effort. In 1964 the two parties spent almost $35 million in the Presidential race. The cost of Senate races may be nominal in non-competitive States, but in 1966 Kenneth Keating and Robert Kennedy each put out at least $2 million in New York. House campaign costs also vary greatly, from about $10,000 for "safe" seats to at least $100,000 when the competition is keen.

Until about 1956 the cost of campaigning apparently was rising pretty much in line with the cost of living, but thereafter campaign costs took a giant leap, largely because of the increased use of television. Thus in 1964 the two Presidential candidates together spent $4.1 million for television time, and in 1968 Nixon spent about $5.2 million, while Humphrey had to be content with a measly $3 million. Even those sums seem small in proportion to the report by the Federal Communications Commission that almost $80 million was spent that year in political broadcasts and their preparation; of course, this figure included candidates for lesser offices. There are other costs: campaign planes and trains, hire of auditoriums, bringing of busloads of supporters and, by no means least, frequent, extensive and expensive public opinion polls.

James MacGregor Burns has shown that not only have most of the great urban and State party machines shriveled away, but relatively few individual citizens any longer take a vital interest in working for a party. He attributes these phenom-

---

[1]See especially Alexander Heard, *The Costs of Democracy* (University of North Carolina Press, 1960); Herbert E. Alexander, *Financing the 1960 Election* and *Financing the 1964 Election,* both published in Princeton by the Citizens' Research Foundation; and *The Journal of Politics,* Nov. 1963, which was devoted to political finance. Most of the information given here is taken from Frank J. Sorauf, *Party Politics in America* (Boston: Little, Brown, 1968), pages 300-323, which draws on the previously cited sources.

ena to the way in which the parties fall between three stools—the nation, the States, and the localities. They are called on to fulfill functions so different and to coalesce so many irreconcilable interests that they simply cannot do it. A sweep by a popular national Democratic candidate, as in the case of Franklin Roosevelt, can emasculate the State and local Republican organizations for years. The result is the breakdown of party organizations and the institution of political guerrilla warfarc, in which candidates have to assume responsibility for their own campaigns and finances.

An almost universal feature of campaigns nowadays is seen in Republican candidate Smith's efforts to organize "Democrats for Smith" and Democratic candidate Jones's efforts to organize "Republicans for Jones." Perhaps because the voter has become more sophisticated, party labels in local and State elections, at least below the office of governor, have declined in significance. It is each candidate for himself except where courthouse gangs still exercise a throttle hold. The office holder—especially a member of Congress—can and sometimes does develop national and international interests, but he must give first and greatest attention to his rear, for if he loses the support of the disparate elements in his district and in the State legislature, he will find himself out of a job.

Not only can a Roosevelt affect local political organizations, but the process can be reversed: courthouse gangs and personal organizations, in alliance, can vitally affect State elections. Since the State legislature is responsive to them, it often gerrymanders Congressional districts so that they become safe for one party or the other; the legislature may even divide "safe districts" between the parties. The result is that about half the Congressional districts never shift from one party to another, and about a quarter shift only rarely. Since the holders of safe seats seldom welcome change, any reform movement in the House of Representatives, therefore, must operate on a paper-thin margin. Thus Johnson's Great Society program depended on the forty-odd liberal Congressmen brought in because of the Republican error in nominating Goldwater—and the liberal margin was lost in the election of 1966.

It can be seen from the foregoing that Congress—especially the House—is made up largely of men less concerned with national welfare than with placating local interests. If a Congressman is adept at preserving his local and State base, he can confidently look forward to amassing the seniority that will make him a committee chairman or ranking minority member and political power. It is a gruelling task that requires special aptitudes, and many Congressmen give up in disgust and trade for a judicial office or aim for less exacting State administrative or legislative offices.

No doubt certain deviations in the once highly regarded primary are partly responsible for this breakdown of political distinctions, but we can also lay some blame on voter indifference, or voter hostilities, the breakdown of many urban political machines, and—as previously noted—on voter sophistication. Hitherto, democracy has been more able to "throw the rascals out"—that is, try to prevent any further errors—than to initiate new policies. Nowadays voters, at least the young, are no longer content with a veto after the fact, but want to share in making policy. Thus far we have not found a good way to do this. No one has yet come up with a reasonable alternative to the two local and State methods of selecting candidates—the primary and the convention—but no doubt either of them can be refined, formalized, and made more expressive of real public opinion. At the same time it should be recognized that, with all their faults, it is the local political organizations (along with the numerous church, social, do-gooder, and special interest organizations) that give to our political system much of whatever stability it possesses. They form mass opinion, and mass opinion, as V. O. Key says, possesses a high viscosity.

Obviously, then, the causes of the breakdown of parties are many. One need not stop with the factors mentioned above, nor with the Vietnam War, nor with the influx of eighteen-year-olds who are not impressed by either the hardships their elders faced or the problems they solved. Technology plays a role in politics that is seldom recognized. Hundreds of thousands of Southern Negroes went north during World War II to work in industries. The mechanization of cotton culture and picking destroyed the chief means by which millions of Southern blacks earned a living and sent them flocking to Northern cities; the prospect of a similar revolution in tobacco culture is likely to accelerate the movement. At the same time, and often for the same reason, Southern white tenant farmers poured into Northern cities, carrying their race antipathies with them.

As the core cities were increasingly populated by blacks and Southern whites, affluent whites and the better-paid blue-collar workers fled to the suburbs, followed by many industries. This eroded the cities' tax bases so greatly that they were unable to furnish satisfactory public services or pay city workers adequately. The result was a vicious spiral of discontent, strikes, riots, crime, and racial strife. The white suburbs refused to join in solving the cities' problems and, moreover, the more affluent blacks began to move out of the cities into the suburbs. In fact, by 1970 the suburbs had come to outrank the adjacent cities in population—even New York City, if one considers the adjacent areas in New York, Connecticut, and New Jersey. We now have to deal with cities that are bankrupt, decaying, and torn by lawlessness and racial strife.

Political parties had long depended for support on city political machines, but the change in the makeup of urban population eroded the foundations of the machines; probably also a factor in this erosion was that the machines no longer performed their old function of helping the poor. Moreover, blatant corruption now promoted cynicism among voters, either because they were disappointed at not sharing the spoils or because they expected a higher standard of civic administration. At any rate, the effect was to hasten the breakup of the Roosevelt political coalition, which depended partly on city machines.

The once reliably Democratic South may now be in the process of going over to the Republican Party. One reason, of course, is the public school desegregation decision by the Supreme Court in 1954, but is it too much to say that the decision was at least in part the result of the political pressure of black voters in the Northern cities, and so had its origin in the cotton-picking machine? In pointing out the above considerations, Samuel Lubell expresses the opinion that in 1968 the country was so divided on issues of ideology and self-interest that it would have been split into antagonistic parts by any possible presidential candidate, especially Robert Kennedy.[2]

WHAT CAN BE DONE TO RENOVATE THE PARTY SYSTEM?

Now of course anyone except the entrenched politicians and their cohorts would agree that the situation is so unhealthy that it actually prevents the flexibility so essential to progress, perhaps even to national survival. What can be done about it?

Back in the 1940's E. E. Schattschneider chaired a committee of the American Political Science Association that in 1950 issued a significant report on how to reconstruct the party system and make it more effective.[3] The committee:

1. Advised the general adoption of the "closed primary"—that is, every voter would register as a member of one party and in the primary election could vote only for those seeking to be candidates of that party.

2. Preferred the "short ballot," which means that only a few officials should be elected, so that the voters could keep a close watch on them and their appointees and hold them strictly responsible for their performances.

3. Recommended the abolition of the anachronistic Electoral College, with its system of "winner takes all" in each state.

4. Made suggestions for raising campaign finances.

5. Asked for the publication annually by the Bureau of the Census of a volume giving detailed statistical, biographical, historical, and election data.

6. Proposed that national Presidential nominating conventions be limited to 300 to 350 elected delegates who, with ex officio members, would bring the number to not more than 500 to 600 members.

7. Recommended that national conventions meet biennially and set up a national party council, which would be continuously active in setting policies and coordinating relations among national, State, and local party organizations.

8. Proposed that candidates be bound by the party platform, and that the platform state a permanent, long-range philosophy.

---

[2]Samuel Lubell, in *The Hidden Crisis in American Politics* (New York: Norton, 1970), analyzes the present political situation. On the above see especially pages 64 and 287 ff.

[3]American Political Science Association, Committee on Political Parties, *Toward a More Responsible Two-Party System* (New York: Rinehart, 1950); also published as a *Supplement* to *American Political Science Review*, xliv, no. 3, part 2 (Sept. 1950).

9. Demanded that the party control its Congressmen by eliminating those Congressional procedures (such as the seniority system) that destroy party responsibility.

10. Emphasized that party organization should be given more form by attracting dues-paying members who would share in molding policies and would be active in compaigns.

A further problem in our political system is that many times elections to local, state, and national offices occur on the same day, so that in most cases a man holding one elective office cannot bid for another without giving up the office he has. Thus the members of the lower House in a State or in Washington often stake their political careers when they bid for higher office; so, too, a Governor or a Senator often risks unemployment when he seeks a different office—and, moreover, the State or the nation may lose his services for at least two years.

Milton C. Cummings, in *Congressmen and the Electorate* (1966), examined at considerable length the mutual impact of Presidential and Congressional candidates. He found that many incumbent Congressmen had a good chance of surviving even when the Presidential candidate of their party was defeated; whether that will be true after the redistricting decreed by the Supreme Court remains to be seen. Cummings also found that when Congressmen were elected at large—that is, when all the voters of the state voted for undistricted Congressmen—the result tended to approach the vote given the party's Presidential candidate. The interdependence between Presidential and Congressional candidates of the same party was heightened.

This suggests that districts be enlarged so as to have several Congressmen, and that each party run its candidates on an "at large" ticket, with each voter entitled to as many votes as there are candidates but allowed to cast only one vote for a single candidate, though he could divide his votes between the parties. In this way the minority party would be likely to obtain better representation in all regions than it gets now. Each candidate should thus receive adequate exposure before the electorate and make it possible for the voters to follow and assess the career of each man after he is elected. The usefulness of this method is suggested by the way in which the Senate, since popular election was instituted, has become more representative of popular and national opinion than the locally oriented House. Certainly some way must be found to cut the umbilical cord between Congressmen and the local machines.

PROPOSALS FOR A UNICAMERAL CONGRESS

The renovation of the party system is, in my opinion, so bound up with the technical aspects of our Constitution and our customary procedures that this is probably the best place to give a short preview of the more technical parts of my recommendaticns.

I have already outlined in chapter 4 a plan for the consolidation of States, proposing that their boundaries be no longer sacrosanct and that State sovereignty be abandoned in exchange for the duty of administering many present-day Federal functions with a minimum of Federal guidelines. I propose that the House of Representatives become a unicameral legislature, to be called Congress, and that the President be its de facto leader, with a limited power to dissolve it and call for a new election when he and Congress arrive at an impasse.

The reconstituted Congress, which would exercise most of the powers of legislation, would consist of 200 elected members not less than twenty-five years of age, serving normally for five-year terms. They would be elected without regard to residence requirements, though after election they should be legal residents of the districts they represent.

Why only 200 members? For a number of reasons. There would be enough significant administrative and committee assignments to go around and to give every member a sense of participation, something that is now often lacking. There would also be room for a number of additional Congressmen-at-Large and Congressmen-pro-Forma, terms I shall presently explain. In any case, with fewer Congressmen representing any given area, it should be possible for the people to watch their performances; indeed, they should be as much in the popular eye as a Senator is now.

I state elsewhere that, by turning more functions over to the enlarged and reconstituted States, the Congressmen should be relieved of some of the local pressures and demands that now make them responsive to special local interests rather than to national interests. I do not mean that a Congressman from Deseret should have no interest in his region's water problem, but I do mean that if Deseret as a State were in a position to handle its water problem as its peculiar conditions dictate, the Congressman would be freer to see Deseret as one of five or six States with water problems and so would be able to take a larger view. As stated above, the Senate, originally envisioned as the champion of big property and States' rights, has now become more representative of popular and national opinion than the locally oriented House. The reason, of course, is that Senators are now popularly elected by the people of their States as a whole, and so represent a much wider constituency than do Representatives.

This suggests that the election of Congressmen by larger districts should free them, at least in part, from local trammels. First of all, I would take control of Federal elections and districting out of the hands of the States. Let Congress set the qualifications of voters, and the Senate, reconstituted as I shall presently suggest, establish uniform rules for the governance of primaries, elections, and their financing, and provide for elected Party Councils in each State composed at least partly of men and women who are not otherwise office holders, though certain State officers might be ex officio members. Of course, every State should have at least one Congressman, but, as stated above, those States large enough to have more than one Congressman should elect them on a general ticket, each voter having as many votes as his State has Congressmen but casting only one vote for a single candidate.

When a State has a considerable number of Congressmen—say more than seven—it should be divided into districts, each with four or whenever possible, five Congressmen, elected on a general ticket. The reconstituted Senate should provide uniform rules for financing primaries and Congressional races but, to preserve party discipline, the campaign expenses should be channeled through the party's central Congressional committee.

The general ticket method of election should ensure that the minority party in a district receives representation. The objection may be made, indeed, that it would encourage the multiplication of minority parties. I think not, for reasons I shall soon advance. But it is essential to the vitality and flexibility of a political system that political mavericks be given a chance to get into Congress. The nomination and election laws should be so formulated as to permit independent candidates to enter primaries and, if nominated, to run in the Congressional election. But if they are elected, and even if they are then accepted as members of a party caucus, they should not be allowed to hold party office during any term for which they were elected as independents. The reason is simple enough: there should be a way for mavericks to get into Congress, but it would be destructive of party discipline to reward them otherwise until they are willing to run as regulars. But in any case the uniform regulations for financing primary and Congressional races should aid them.

I would suggest also that under the above plan a score of mavericks might organize their own party though, as I will later show, it would operate under some handicaps—as it should. Nevertheless, if they have a good cause, history shows that it will be taken up by one of the majority parties—again, as it should be. I know of no better way to keep the major parties from ossifying.[4]

Finally, the demarcation of Congressional districts should not be the work of Congress itself, but of the Senate which, as I shall presently describe it, should be as nearly non-partisan as possible. Moreover, the dates of Federal and State elections should never coincide, so that a valuable State or Federal legislator or official can seek office at the other level without having to give up his current office in case of defeat.

PROPOSALS FOR THE PRESIDENCY

Let us turn next to the manner of electing a President. There is at present a great deal of criticism of the Electoral College, and it is justified: a powerful

---

[4]For a discussion of whether the "single-member district and plurality vote device" encourages the two-party or the multi-party system, see Allan P. Sindler, *Political Parties in the United States* (New York: St. Martin's Press, 1966), page 50ff.

third-party candidate, by his threat to throw the election into the House, can send shivers of apprehension throughout the nation. It has been advocated that we select candidates by means of a national primary, and then in the general election give the office to the man who receives the plurality of votes. This would dispose of the Electoral College, but it would preserve the antagonism between President and Congress; indeed, the antagonism might be worsened, for there is no guarantee that the public would not choose someone quite inexperienced in politics and administration. I for one failed to see the joke when a recent motion picture portrayed the election of a youthful pop singer as President.

The national convention was adopted in the first place to iron out differences within the party and to form a united front in the ensuing campaign. Congressmen are prominent contenders for the Presidential nomination, but so also are Governors of States and members of party councils who have been living in the public eye or successfully solving problems of national significance. Very few delegates come to a convention to sacrifice their political future in defense of a man or a measure. The pressures are always for accommodation, and a certain amount of horse trading is inevitable—as it must always be if democracy is to work. True, the convention is often noisy and even ridiculous, but it does enable partisans to blow off steam; and it provides a means for molding a platform that promotes party unity and for selecting candidates reasonably acceptable to most elements in the party.

V. O. Key considered the national convention an impressive political achievement because it furnishes "an instrumentality for weaving together the diverse and geographically scattered elements of each part into a national whole" and because it "provides a channel for advancement to the Presidency independent of the Congress, a channel that can probably be navigated by men who could not make their way to the top through Congress and that probably is closed to others who can achieve leadership in Congress."[5]

One change I propose is that Presidential campaigns be restricted to 90 days. The six- to nine-month campaigns now in vogue not only are exhausting to the candidates and their aides but eventually bore the electorate. Besides, they are unnecessary in the day of the airplane and television. But I would hate to see the national conventions abolished. These quadrennial orgies may be less disastrous in this century than the enemies of the institution would have us believe. As was pointed out in the last chapter, conventions sometimes nominate weak men— Bryan, Parker, and Davis, who lost; and Harding and Coolidge, who won—but they are well balanced by most of the Presidents who have held office and by candidates who lost—Hughes, Smith, Landon, Willkie, Dewey, and Stevenson. Indeed, the convention system has done quite as well in this century as the parliamentary system in Britain. Moreover, conventions normally have a purga-

---

[5]V. O. Key, *Politics, Parties, and Pressure Groups* (New York: Crowell, 1969), page 443.

tive effect on party obstructionists, and they stir up the political blood, which has become sluggish during the preceding four years.

The problem here is not so much to compare the degree of democracy in the various methods of selecting Presidential candidates, as to promote the more effective implementation of democracy by suggesting a way of getting President and Congress to cooperate. For one thing, each party—by law, if necessary—should hold an annual convention, even if limited to the party councils, to review the party's programs and policies. But the grand convocation should still be the national Presidential nominating convention, with its delegates selected and its rules established by law. In addition to the elected delegates, the party's council, members of Congress, and candidates for Congress should be members, so that the primaries for selecting Congressional candidates would have to precede the selection of convention delegates.

The business of the convention should be to formulate a program and nominate a Presidential candidate, and support of both should be binding on all Congressional candidates. It can be objected that a national nominating convention might choose a Presidential candidate unsatisfactory to Congress, even one sure to stir up controversy with Congress. It could happen; even parliamentary governments at times have elected premiers with whom they could not get along. On the other hand, Congressmen have always been powerful factors in conventions—indeed, they have sometimes been charged with nominating weak Presidential candidates whom they could manage.

This can be expected when the Constitution makes natural enemies of President and Congress. If, however, Congressmen, party councils, and State officials could put forward their real leaders as candidates, they should sometimes be able to sell them to the conventions. This is not cynicism, but realism, for it is simply impossible for the massive membership of a party to act wisely and efficiently without leadership, and whence could the leadership better come than from among those elected to handle political affairs?

The office of Vice-President should be abolished, for recent attempts to give the Vice-President a role in administration have only resulted in damaging the images of men who possessed the potential for national leadership.

Inevitably someone will hark back to King Caucus, previously mentioned as the custom between 1796 and 1824 of nominating Presidential candidates in meetings of partisan Congressmen. Also as previously noted, it was not a bad system if one can judge by the men nominated—much better than the record set by most conventions during the rest of the century. The caucus was opposed on the ground that the legislative branch should not choose the executive—a logical objection in the light of the Constitution's separation of powers. But this objection can no longer hold unless there is a deliberate and mulish intention to obstruct governmental processes.

An integral part of my proposal is that no votes be cast for the Presidential candidate as such, but that the party electing the plurality of Congressmen also win the Presidency. If perchance two parties tie, then the one with the larger popular vote gets the Presidency.

But how can a party carry on government when it does not have a majority of the Congressmen? My proposal is that the newly elected President be empowered to appoint enough Congressmen-at-Large to bring his Congressional majority up to 55%. This is not likely to happen very often, unless a third and rather powerful party is in the field, and even this condition has had very little effect thus far. In the 53 elections of the House of Representatives from 1866 to 1968 inclusive, the plurality party has failed only 17 times to win 55% or more and even then, so far as I can find, always won over 50%. (Of course, this is not as important as it looks in view of the Bourbon-Old Guard Alliance and the split between Presidential and Congressional parties; moreover, the admission of new States and deaths among members before Congress actually met sometimes changed the balance slightly.)

In the event that two parties each elected 100 Congressmen the Chief Justice would authorize the President to appoint a sufficient number of Congressmen-at-Large to provide his party in the Congress a 55% majority. The total voting membership in the Congress would also be raised by that number.[6] To limit his control over his appointees the President would not be permitted to remove them. He would, however, be permitted to appoint successors in the event of death, resignation, or removal by Congressional action. In the event several parties elected Congressmen the Chief Justice would similarly authorize the President to appoint a sufficient number of Congressmen-at-Large to raise the plurality party in Congress to the desired 55% majority.[7]

In many cases President and Congress would serve out their five-year terms, but it is conceivable that by-elections (special elections to fill seats vacated by death or resignation) would gradually change the complexion of Congress or that there would arise an irremediable difference between the President and his party or a dissident element within the party. True, the President might be ousted by Congress, or even by his party caucus, but a caucus is much more likely to seek

---

[6]The number of Presidential appointees would be calculated in accordance with the formula:

$$\frac{.45}{100} \text{ x } \frac{.55}{x}$$

Where "x" represents the number of members needed to produce a 55% majority. In this example x = 123 (122.2 rounded). The total membership would become 100 + 123 or 223.

[7]Assuming that the plurality party elected 90 members and the other parties elected 60, 40, and 10 respectively (110 total) the formula would be applied as follows:

$$\frac{.45}{110} \text{ x } \frac{.55}{x}$$

In this case the President would be authorized to appoint 45 Congressmen-at-Large (x = 135 - 90 = 45). The voting membership would be raised to 245.

an accommodation than to risk a snap election, especially if computerization offers proof that a particular decision is best.

THE "LOYAL OPPOSITION"

At this point I wish to introduce a proposal intended to give continuous leadership and experience to the defeated party or parties. I would provide for yet a third category of Congressmen, who for lack of a better name I call Congressmen-pro-Forma. First among them I would include former Presidents, but in addition each Congressional party that elects at least 20% of the Constitutional 200 would be entitled to appoint as many as fifteen of its leaders not members of Congress, including defeated Presidential candidates, who would exercise all the rights, privileges, and duties of elected Congressmen except the right to vote on the floor.

By permitting certain defeated party leaders to enter Congress without vote we should prevent the serious waste of leadership that follows nearly all national campaigns and was so poignantly illustrated by the fate of Adlai Stevenson, and give continual national exposure and experience to potential leaders. If a man is good enough to head a major party, let alone serve a term in the Presidency, there ought to be a way to continue to use his talents. Moreover, providing for such memberships would encourage the rise in each minority party of a "Shadow Cabinet" (after the British example), which would be working continually on alternative policies. Thus it would be possible for an incoming President (or at least his Cabinet) to be on top of the job immediately, without the ten or eleven weeks of frantic study now essential. In a time of crisis there may well be a vital need for the speedy transfer of power. Finally, and by no means unimportant, the creation of Congressmen-pro-Forma would provide a means of introducing promising new blood to the national scene.

To me, the virtue of the above proposals is that they combine the outstanding features of the American and British systems. The present American contest system means that the winner takes all, whether he be Presidential or Congressional candidate. True, a senior Senator or Representative may take a new man under his wing, as Sam Rayburn did Lyndon Johnson, but even then the man must prove his worth by hard work, respect for his elders, and observance of the rule "To get along, go along." But most important, he must show the ability to get re-elected—again—and again—and again.

The British-sponsored system consciously seeks out promising young men and runs them for Parliament; if they lose and their promise is great enough, the next time around they are assigned to run in a "safe" constituency. No system is or can be perfect, but the British have and deserve to have more intelligent leaders than we have—men who are purposefully trained in the various aspects of the Parliamentary Establishment, and who can look forward to a continuous and honorable career in public life.

PROPOSALS FOR A RECONSTITUTED SENATE

It remains to consider the Senate, for which I would propose a new role. The presiding officer of the Senate would be the Chief Justice, elected for five years by the Senate, and he would appoint courts and committees with the consent of the Senate. He would also serve as titular Head of State and assume administrative powers when there was no President. I would limit the body normally to 100, half of them lawyers (Law Senators) appointed by the President, with the consent of Congress, from slates drawn up by the States. The Chief Justice would receive from any source nominations of the remaining Senators (Senators-at-Large, not learned in the law), and the Senate would screen them and submit a slate of candidates to Congress, which would consider the nominations *in camera* and elect them by secret ballot.

Senators would be thirty-five years of age or more and would serve for life or until the age of seventy. The Senate would combine judicial and investigative duties, would serve as a national ombudsman, and would have the right to suspend Presidential orders or Congressional legislation for six months. It would also have the right to introduce legislation into Congress and, in case of a prolonged impasse, to dissolve Congress and call a new election. The Law Senators would constitute the various courts of last resort, supervise lower Federal courts—and in some cases State courts—and would set up permanent courts or commissions whose funtion would be to protect the rights of the citizen. Questions of constitutionality, however, would be determined by the entire Senate. Senators-at-Large would devote themselves chiefly to investigation of Congressional legislation, to delineating Congressional districts, to oversight of political procedures, and to supervising the expenditure of campaign funds—and probably furnishing them from the public treasury. Of course, all non-judicial decisions would be made in the end by the entire Senate.

Chapter 7

THE PRESIDENT AND THE CONGRESS

POMP AND CIRCUMSTANCE

Thus far I have presented the President as severely handicapped by the jealousies of House and Senate and limited by the not always strictly Constitutional activities of the Supreme Court. Nevertheless, he is often portrayed as the most powerful executive in the world—certainly not the figurehead that we see in the Soviet Union and a number of other countries.

He is a busy man. By throwing out the first baseball of the season he inaugurates the great American game. He buys the first Christmas seals, is photographed with the sweet and rather pathetic children who are chosen to symbolize the drives against certain diseases. He pins medals on heroes or on Gold Star mothers, and he discourses with earnest but half-baked young idealists in the rose garden. He entertains the entire House and Senate at a series of breakfasts or (it is rumored) has some members in for cozy chats by the fireside. He gives official balls and stands in receiving lines shaking hands until his fingers bleed. He receives visiting dignitaries from abroad, wines and dines them, then goes into huddles during which only heaven and the interpreters know what is said— probably nothing of moment, if the official communiques are to be trusted.

He can't move without an entourage of Secret Service men—nor can any member of his family—for no one knows when some deranged person lies in wait with a telescope-equipped rifle or a hand grenade. He must listen to the obscenities of new-style protesters who congregate outside the rose garden or carry signs just outside the iron fence on Pennsylvania Avenue, led not only by whiskered and beaded fanatics but by elderly preachers and medicos to whom God has delivered the secret of how to save the world.

As if all this were not enough, we insist, with true Anglo-Saxon logic, that he combine two utterly irreconcilable roles—chief of his party and President of *all* the people. He must be at one and the same time the symbol of unity and the hallmark of disunity. It is no wonder that he inevitably falls between two stools, and that at least half of the thinking population oppose or at least deplore him. Sometimes the President seems to be as confused and ambivalent as the citizens.

A President has a hard life and far from a merry one, despite the helicopter and Air Force One waiting to whisk him away to his mountain or beach hideaways. Perhaps the only really rewarding moments are when he descends the grand staircase with the First Lady on his arm and the band bursts into "Hail to the Chief Who in Triumph Advances."

The physical and psychological burdens are so crushing that an ordinary mortal cannot help wondering if any man who wishes to be President is sane enough to be entrusted with the task. This is not an idle thought, for ambitious men often have a Caesar lying within. The danger is all the greater in these days when far-flung crises, faithless allies, mindless dissenters on left and right, striking civil servants, one-track generals and admirals, organized criminals, and obstructive legislators seem determined to stymie even the most ordinary processes of government.

It is time to state that my proposal does not envision an "all-powerful" President and Congress. It is all very well for the British Constitution to be exactly whatever the House of Commons says it is, for self-restraint is an innate part of the British character—or at least so it is said. But when the British concept of the Constitution is transferred to South Africa, it quickly becomes a means of tightening the noose of tyranny. And if the last few decades have proved anything, they have shown that we need Constitutional checks and balances, though not necessarily those set up in 1787. Here let me quote part of the preamble to my proposed new Constitution.

> The government of the United States shall be vested in a Congress, and in a judiciary headed by a Senate, and such officials as they Constitutionally select or provide for. These shall be, among others, a Chief Justice of the United States who serves as Chief of State under the oversight of the Senate, and a President who acts as the executive arm of the Congress under the legislative oversight of the Congress and the judicial and investigatory oversight of the Senate.

The concentration of so much power in a President has given the office an awesomeness which also invests the man who holds it. Inevitably he loses contact with public opinion, for he has time neither to read periodicals and current books, to confer in depth with his advisers or with Congressmen, nor to sit back and really think. His isolation even makes it impossible for him to assess properly the strength of the opposition, in either Congress or the nation; witness the puzzlement of Lyndon Johnson over the opposition to his Vietnam War policy, a feeling which presently turned to anger and finally to frustration so deep that he decided not to run again for the Presidency. In a sense, everyone with whom the President comes in contact is a yes-man, for no one is going to act as devil's advocate—at least persistently—in the face of the awesomeness of the office. Moreover, Presidents show a tendency to get rid of anyone who does not, in effect, butter them up.

Now of course this is not necessarily true obsequiousness on the part of the White House aides and Cabinet Secretaries, for anyone who comprehends the burdens of the office should sincerely desire to avoid making them worse by pushing too hard on matters distasteful to the President. But this is not invariably the case. Any President will have not only sycophants but secret enemies in his entourage. Vice-President Charles G. Dawes once remarked that the "members of the Cabinet are a President's natural enemies." Probably there is no way to escape this condition, for we see it in British Cabinets, where the senior Cabinet members are rivals of the Prime Minister. But in public the British Cabinet presents a united front, which an American Cabinet does not. Certainly there is a growing tendency for Cabinet members to undercut Administration policy, and sometimes openly to show disloyalty. This helps explain why the President has installed in the White House a Kitchen Cabinet, which has almost if not fully displaced the Cabinet Secretaries as an advisory council. This has proved to be a source of irritation between the President and his personal staff on one hand and the Cabinet on the other. Even Congress resents these persons, and regards them as janizaries set to prevent access to the President.

It is true that much of the criticism of Presidential power now comes from men who formerly favored it, but have changed their minds—at least temporarily—because of the Vietnam War. Nevertheless, circumstances almost force the President further away from an understanding of the public desire and of political reality and weaken his power to educate and lead the public. He is coming more and more to present a public image of being dictatorial if not actually wishing to become a dictator.[1]

BRINGING THE PRESIDENCY DOWN TO REALITY

My proposal that the powers of the Presidency be split among a Chief Justice, a President, a Congress, and a Senate derives in large part from the hope that it would ameliorate the conditions noted above. The Presidency would lose much

---

[1]These and other ideas are explored by Arthur Schlesinger, Jr., in *The Crisis of Confidence: Ideas, Power, and Violence in America* (New York: Houghton Mifflin, 1969). For books on the Presidency, see the footnote on page 66.

of its awesomeness, and the President would be forced to become aware of public opinion and political realities simply because he could no longer hide behind a Kitchen Cabinet but would have to deal directly with Congress—in fact, be a part of it, share its fortunes, and be forced to shape his ideas and policies by contact with a group of men who would not be overawed by him or his office. Failure on his part to whet his ideas and policies on the hones not only of his colleagues but of the opposition would result in his being ousted from office. Furthermore, such a system is the best way to assure that the President would educate and lead the public instead of passing down commandments from Mount Sinai.

The objective, therefore, should be to confirm that the President is a member of Congress, its presiding officer, and *chief of the executive arm of Congress.* He would lose the right to veto bills, but his actions would never require approval by more than a majority of Congress.

As was mentioned in Chapter 5, the long friction between President and Congress was one of the factors in the creation by the latter of quasi-judicial agencies, such as the Interstate Commerce Commission, intended to bypass the executive. This practice should be stopped or severely restricted, perhaps by permitting such agencies to exist only by the consent of the reconstituted Senate. Executive functions should be divided among the members of an official Cabinet, appointed and removable by the President from among the voting members of Congress—that is, from elected Congressmen or Congressmen-at-Large.

Moreover, Cabinet officers should have enough deputies to relieve them of their present crushing burdens and give them time to be real Presidential advisers and mediators in Congress, along with the usual party floor leaders. These deputies could be drawn from any of the three categories of Congressmen or, if appointed from outside, should become Congressmen-pro-Forma as long as they retain their positions. It is to be hoped that there would be a greater degree of Cabinet and Sub-Cabinet cohesion and loyalty than there is at present.

THE ROLE OF CONGRESSIONAL COMMITTEES

The committee system is so deeply entrenched in Congress that it probably could not be excised—nor should be. The burden of legislative business is so enormous that it could not be handled in any other way. The committee, at least in theory, serves three indispensable functions: it is the receptacle into which flows the needed technical and political information and the views of various interest groups; it publicizes, we can hope, all aspects of a matter at issue; and it irons out differences and shapes a legislative bill.

Hitherto committees have had to build up their own staffs of experts in order to avoid becoming creatures of the bureaucracy. The result often is that individual legislators may become experts in the work with which their committee deals; sometimes they become so valuable that when they lose an election they may be retained on the committee's staff. My proposal that there be Congressmen-at-

Large and Congressmen-pro-Forma is made partially to prevent the loss of this hard-won expertise, and to continue the training of such men for future administrative positions.

The flaws of the committee system lie in the seniority rule and in the independence of the members from party control, even after the party decision is made —if it is made. In the short space available it is impossible to explain the complexities of legislation in the Congress. It is sufficient to say that, though the Congressional mill grinds out legislation even as the fabled salt mill grinds out salt at the bottom of the sea, there is a paucity of vital and carefully considered legislation.

The three functions of the Congressional committee named above are more theoretical than actual. Samuel P. Huntington found that both Houses of Congress have become institutionalized. After about four terms as a Representative, a man has to leave for another pasture or decide to make a career exclusively in the House; save in exceptional cases every other avenue of leadership is closed to him. He may go into State politics or into the Senate, but if he becomes a Senator he finds that he has exchanged one treadmill for another: Taft, Knowland, Goldwater, and Humphrey found it impossible to move to the Presidency; and Harding, Johnson, and Nixon made it by what now seem to be flukes. Kennedy was never a part of the Senate Establishment, but deliberately used his position—along with the family wealth—to boost himself into the Presidency.

Long service in House or Senate, then, almost automatically bars one from other fields of public service. Only rarely does a President reach into Congress for a Cabinet member, and only rarely do Cabinet members go into Congress. Huntington showed that in 1963 about 77% of the leaders of Congress were living in the States of their birth, while 70% of administration leaders were living *outside* the States of their birth. Senators and Representatives typically came from rural backgrounds, while administration leaders normally came from cities. Even Congressmen sympathetic to business think of it in small-town terms and are often uneasy about big corporations.

The foregoing facts help explain why Congress is stymied by the twentieth century and why President, Cabinet, and bureaucracy have had to take over what is essentially the legislative function. Deplorable as it may seem to some observers, businessmen and corporation lawyers are continually passing in and out of the administration and doing something to keep it at least reasonably abreast of the times—as well, it is to be suspected, as serving corporate interests. Legislative bills now typically originate in administration offices. Congressional leaders, with some few exceptions, are no longer molders of policy. With their eyes always fixed on the local bosses back home and their fellow satraps in Congress, they have become insulated from the nation as a whole and from world currents. Moreover, they are so bedeviled for services by the folks back home that they have little time to study proposed legislation or sit down and think a problem through.

Huntington's analysis exposes a situation that has developed through the years and has resulted in what is not far from being a state of legislative paralysis. The initiative in proposing significant legislation has passed to the President; about 80 percent of the bills voted into law originate in the executive branch. On the other hand, Congress has tremendously expanded the number of its investigations—sometimes for good reason, though not always. Theoretically this should enable Congress to serve as a sort of ombudsman and, indeed, as the bureaucracy comes more and more to represent powerful special interests, the value of Congressional investigations to the common citizen becomes greater.[2]

THE NECESSITY OF COOPERATION

It should now be clear why I would lay stress on cooperation among President, Cabinet, bureaucracy, and Congressional committees. If Congress is to survive as a legislative agency, it must renovate its committee functions and assure an administrative future for ambitious younger members. Congress does not need to surrender either its legislative or investigatory powers, but it does need to rationalize and modernize them. This is another reason I have proposed that the President or his deputies take a serious part in the work of Congressional committees. Computerization, as I have indicated, may help promote this objective.

The President should not only be the presiding officer of Congress (hence his title), though that function would undoubtedly be exercised by a deputy drawn from the voting members of Congress, but he should also be ex officio chairman of all Congressional committees. Here again the function would normally be carried on by deputies; in the case of committees dealing primarily with the affairs of a given Cabinet Department, the Cabinet Secretary should be vice-chairman.

The President's role as ex officio chairman of all committees is to enable him to ensure party regularity, but he would nevertheless be subject to the party caucus, and to Congress as a whole. Even Presidential appointments not subject to Congressional approval would be open to criticism in caucus, and if the President ignored its opinion too often, he would risk its displeasure. He would need its support to strike out riders, rippers (i.e., a bill which alters administrative organization in order to gain partisan advantage by abolishing offices held by the opposition), clauses in pending bills, and items in appropriation bills, and to bypass the present obstructive process by which funds must be authorized and appropriated by separate bills considered by separate committees—in both the House and the Senate! He should also have the right to strike out ripper clauses sneaked into bills and intended to repeal previous legislation.

---

[2]Huntington, "Congressional Responses to the Twentieth Century," in The American Assembly (D. B. Truman, ed.), *The Congress and America's Future* (Englewood Cliffs, N.J.: Prentice-Hall, 1965), pages 23-25. On the other hand, Congress and bureaucracy may try to delay decisions and fuzz issues by appointing investigating commissions. As stated on a previous page, one estimate has it that there are 3,000 commissions at the Federal level, not to mention those in State and local governments.

Later I shall propose certain checks that could be exercised by the Senate on President and Congress, but the President's real concern within Congress should be more than keeping the good will of his party caucus—his concern should be to guide the caucus and to influence public opinion. True, through his control of the party's central Congressional committee he would control the campaign funds so essential in Congressional elections, and with the consent of the caucus he would appoint the majority members of committees. Nevertheless, the President could lose the support of the caucus, for on petition of a third of the voting members of the caucus, decisions would have to be taken by secret ballot. Defeat of the President on very many such votes, and certainly defeat on a vote of confidence (whether open or secret) by the caucus would have to result in his resignation.

In case of the President's death, resignation for private reasons, or removal by impeachment and conviction, Congress would elect a successor to fill out the term. In case of a stalemate between President and Congress or his defeat in a vote of confidence by Congress or the majority caucus, the President would have the right to call for national conventions and elections that would initiate a new quinquennium. However, if the President were forced to resign under a cloud of incompetence or scandal and, in the opinions of three-quarters of the Congress, did not deserve further consideration, he would not be permitted to demand an election. This could be a more or less quiet substitute for the prolonged process of examination for insanity or of impeachment and trial for high crimes and misdemeanors. More than likely, the decision to get rid of an irrational or criminal President would be basically political rather than medical or juristic. The present Twenty-Fifth Amendment is not only complicated but couched in such obscure terms that it probably is not enforceable.

The system I propose is a modified version of the Cabinet or Parliamentary form, but I have sought to find ways to avoid multi-party deadlocks and the power of the British prime minister to dissolve Parliament for purely political motives —that is, whenever in his judgment the electorate is favorably disposed to return him to office. And, as I have earlier sought to show, national Presidential nominating conventions have their uses.

Objectors to the parliamentary form of government usually cite countries where parliamentarianism is a mere travesty: where there is no provision for a workable majority, perhaps because of an unwise slavishness to proportional representation—which encourages the multiplication of parties; where President and Premier share executive powers—a plainly impossible situation; or where the executive can be ousted on almost any pretext, however trivial. Properly conceived and honestly carried out, parliamentarianism is more responsive to the public will and more flexible in meeting changing conditions than any other democratic system. And these facts, it may as well be said, are exactly the reasons why certain elements in this country oppose its institution.

Chapter 8

THE JUDICIAL SYSTEM

APPOINTMENT OF SENATORS

The proposals in the preceding chapters are made on the assumption that the burden of the Presidency as at present constituted is too heavy for one man, and that there should be an official in a non-political position to bear part of the burden. The title borne by this official may be of secondary significance, but I prefer "Chief Justice" for two reasons. One is that I would amalgamate the Supreme Court and the Senate into the highest court in the land, to be final arbiter on questions of Constitutional interpretation. It would be a body devoted to preserving a rational balance among the parts of the Federal government and among Federal, State, and local authorities; to protecting the rights of the citizen; to observing and investigating the functioning of the laws and proposing such new laws and Constitutional amendments as it deems beneficial; and to acting in such other capacities as are specified in the revised Constitution.

My second reason is mainly psychological. Most Americans have been aware of the symbolism of the flag as standing for liberty and justice for all, but have also been aware of the way in which our ideals have been so shamefully violated in practice that in the minds and mouths of many people in this and other lands our flag has become a symbol of tyranny. We should therefore place at the head of the nation an officer whose duty is to see justice done—but to temper justice with mercy—and give him as co-workers in the search for justice a body of men and women chosen for their knowledge, rationality, and moderation.

Where would one find a body of paragons to perform such duties? Obviously, no such body will ever be perfect, but governmental necessities cannot await perfection. It is obvious that judges—even those who do not have to face the elective process periodically—are sometimes motivated by political or ideological factors. For this reason I propose that the Senate be composed of Law Senators to the normal number of fifty, but that they be balanced by fifty Senators-at-Large who are not lawyers.

First let us take up the Law Senators. In theory, membership in the present Supreme Court is a civic honor and duty rather than a political prize, and so it should be with the reconstituted Senate. Originally the Senators were supposed to represent the interests of the States in the Federal structure, and to a considerable extent they still do, though their interest in and knowledge of national and international affairs has outrun that of the House. The new Senate might well perform somewhat the same function by having its Law members selected from the new regional States but without being subservient to local interests, as Senators once were and as Representatives now usually are. But a better reason for giving the new States a voice in their selection would be the Senators' function of preserving a rational balance between States on one side and the Federal government on the other.

The one "entrenched" provision of the Constitution of 1787, in Article V, provides "that no state, without its consent, shall be deprived of its equal suffrage in the Senate." No doubt this was the key proviso that reconciled the small States to the acceptance of the Constitution, and perhaps it is still necessary. It is not likely to be changed without a period of re-education, even if the States were to accept consolidation into regional States as I have proposed.

However, there is no requirement that a Senator be a resident of the State *before* the moment of his election. In fact, Robert Kennedy moved from Massachusetts to New York on the eve of the election of 1964, in which he was elected Senator from the latter State. It is all the more likely that if the Senate sheds its political complexion, a State will look around for men who will bring prestige to it regardless of their residence.

My proposal is that Law Senators be not less than thirty-five years of age and serve until seventy; after that, if the Senate desires, they could be retained for limited terms in auxiliary capacities, such as members of the numerous commissions that will be essential to carry out the functions of the Senate. Law Senators would be selected by Congress (including in this case Congressmen-pro-Forma) from lists composed of lawyers with high legal and juristic qualifications, drawn up in the States by a committee of the Judicial Assembly, a committee of the State's Senate, its executive, and the majority and minority leaders of the legislature. The Congress would have the right to reject any or all the nominees as under-qualified (or perhaps too political), in which case the list would be passed on to the Senate and voted upon. One may assume with some confidence that the

State's nominating committee will do its best to present qualified candidates, even at the cost of reaching outside the State.

Why cannot the lawyers in the present Senate perform the functions I propose for the Senate as a judicial body? My position is not likely to flatter lawyers, but routine legal training is no longer as significant in the legislative process as it once was. Bills are no longer drawn up by Congressmen but by legislative or bureaucratic assistants. Indeed, those members of Congress who are lawyers are more likely to be experienced in drawing up wills and trying misdemeanors than in formulating legislation. Their ignorance—or at least disregard—of civil rights and the rules of evidence has been disgracefully shown in Congressional hearings, and (probably from political opportunism) they have joined joyously in passing such plainly unconstitutional legislation as the McCarran Act of 1950 and the Jenner-Butler Act of 1958. In other words, they usually know little or nothing of the science—or art—of jurisprudence and, even when they do, their training does not necessarily fit them to deal with new conditions for which legal theory or precedent offers no guidance.

A jurist is more than merely "learned in the law"; in addition to legal training he possesses a profound knowledge of the foundations of legal theory and of justice tempered by common sense, and a feeling for what is possible. No one is more aware than he of Solon's dictum that the lawgiver should attempt no more good than the people can bear.

Jurisprudents, then, should have a far more important place in our legal system than run-of-the-mine lawyers or corporation practitioners, and they have been rare in Congress. As a matter of fact, a good liberal education is a better preparation for effective legislative service than a law degree. (I will even go so far as to assert that ultimate decisions on Constitutionality are within the competence of thoughtful and knowledgeable men and women not trained in the law.)

Of course there is no dearth of judicious-minded lawyers in the country, and some of them actually reach the Supreme Court. The tragedy is that all too often the justices are selected for political reasons, and much abler men are passed over. We have had recent illustrations of this when Nixon, ostensibly searching for Southern strict-constructionist justices, passed by Southern judges who not only met the criterion of strict constructionism but were far more distinguished for their juristic wisdom than the men he nominated.

I have already expressed the opinion that even the best legal minds are not always geared to deal with new conditions for which legal theory or precedent offers no guidance. That is why I would balance the Law Senators by Senators-at-Large drawn from the ranks of social, economic, cultural, and scientific specialists and generalists. Moreover, though these would not sit on the law courts of the Senate, they would have votes on everything else, including decisions on Constitutionality and suspension of the laws in times of crisis. Since the Senate would have to deal with an ever-increasing burden of extra-legal matters (including laws bearing on matters in which even the best jurists have no expertise) they should be invaluable—as, for example, in numerous fields of investigation.

How should these Senators-at-Large be chosen? My recommendation is that nominations should be quietly received by the Chief Justice from any source, public or private, and that, after due consideration by a Senate screening committee composed in largest part of Senators-at-Large, a slate be drawn up of no fewer than three candidates for each vacancy. The slate would then be considered *in camera* by Congress and selections made by secret ballot of the entire body, including Congressmen-pro-Forma. The selectees should be men and women chosen not only for their expertise—for experts are often wrong—but for rationality, moderation, understanding of humanity's nature and problems, and dedication not so much to ideals that we have often parochially conceived of as American but that ought to be considered in a much broader context as the ideals of all humanity.

This will be a hard thing to do, as we are just beginning to learn from our mistakes in Asia—indeed, over much of the world. Politicians and jurists will have their uses in meeting the future, and so will the popular mandate. But the principal function of our leaders and thinkers must be educational—a function they have never performed satisfactorily in the past, partly at least because they have had to play up to voters and "interests" in order to get elected or reelected.

Any careful observer of the public scene, with a little thought and research, could nominate a score of non-political Americans who would make excellent Senators-at-Large. Though even at its best we cannot expect the Senate to be composed of paragons, we can hope that it will perform its functions with all earnestness, intelligence, and sympathy, tolerably free from unwise political pressures and ready to listen to the voice of reason, good sense, and humanity.

THE PROBLEM OF JUDICIAL REVIEW

Obviously, the proposed composition of the Senate will be a sore subject with lawyers, and it requires some analysis of the actual role played by the Supreme Court and of the evolution of the popular opinion that it is, or should be, sacrosanct. Americans tend to regard the Supreme Court much as ancient Israel regarded the High Priest, the keeper of the ark of the covenant. Over the years the Supreme Court has evolved from a little-regarded judicial body into the guardian of the Constitution and—some say—the keeper of the nation's conscience.

Earlier in this volume reference was made to the fact that for a century each of the three arms of the Federal government claimed the right to interpret the real, inner meaning of the Constitution. Just to complete the record, we should also point out that the States, each in its own way, have claimed the same right. Eminent political scientists and historians have disputed whether the Framers of the Constitution intended to make the Supreme Court the final arbiter of the meaning of the Constitution. Leonard Levy examined the problem and concluded that the disputants sometimes resorted to fallacies, sometimes gave inconsistent data, and sometimes changed their minds.[1]

Edward S. Corwin, one of the above-mentioned disputants, pointed out that the doctrine of judicial review is based on the concept that there is a "universally valid code of justice" and proceeded to tear it down brick by brick. A law professor once remarked that a judge is a law student who grades his own papers. It is not necessary to go quite that far to recognize that judges are fallible—a fact of which the citizen tends to lose sight unless he is haled into court for a misdemeanor; sits on a jury and watches the absurd pass into the asinine à la Charles Dickens's Mr. Bumble; or sees law and order violated with impunity. As it is now, judicial infallibility has become an article of American popular belief, based on the faith that the Founding Fathers settled all Constitutional questions for all time. By and large the justices of the Supreme Court have been inclined to agree. In 1935 Arthur Lippmann satirized this pseudo-ethereal attitude, which was to bring on the court-packing controversy two years later.

> We're nine judicial gentlemen who shun the common herd,
> Nine official mental men who speak the final word.
> We do not issue postage stamps or face the microphones,
> Or osculate with infants, or preside at corner-stones.
> But we're the court of last resort in litigation legal.
> (See: Case of Brooklyn Chicken *versus* Washington Blue Eagle.)
> We never heed the demagogues, their millions and their minions,
> But use *this* handy yard-stick when in doubt about opinions:
>
> > *Chorus*
> > If it's In The Constitution, it's the law,
> > For the Constitution hasn't got a flaw.
> > If it's In The Constitution, it's okay,
> > Whether yesterday, tomorrow, or today—
> > > *Hooray!*
> > If It's In The Constitution, it must stay!
>
> Like oysters in our cloisters, we avoid the storm and strife.
> Some President appoints us, and we're put away for life.
> When Congress passes laws that lack historical foundation,
> We hasten from a huddle and reverse the legislation.
> The sainted Constitution, that great document for students,

---

[1]Leonard W. Levy, "Judicial Review, History, and Democracy," in Levy, ed., *Judicial Review and the Supreme Court: Selected Essays* (New York: Harper and Row, 1967). This valuable little volume, so far as I can see, settles nothing besides demonstrating that Supreme Court justices have been vulnerable to human subjectivities, but that is well worth doing.

Provides an air-tight alibi for all our jurisprudence.
So don't blame us if now and then we seem to act like bounders;
Blame Hamilton and Franklin and the patriotic founders.

Chorus
If it's In The Constitution, it's the law, etc.[2]

Long before this Oliver Wendell Holmes had stated his opinion of judicial infallibility in an off-the-cuff exclamation to an acquaintance: "Young man, I discovered about seventy-five years ago that I wasn't God Almighty!" Right as rain! But what makes anyone believe that a jury of "twelve good men and true" is likely to do anything more than pin a donkey's tail on eternal justice? Juries had their uses in days when judges were little more than arms of executive tyranny and appeals—when the accused could afford them—were not likely to yield any greater measure of justice. Now the jury system has become time-consuming, wasteful of the taxpayers' money, duck soup for eloquent and grand-standing lawyers, and likely to result in half-truths or ludicrous compromises. These objections, it should hastily be added, do not apply to picked grand juries, which have significant investigatory and indicting functions.

But to return to the matter of judicial review, which after the Civil War became an article of American popular faith. Corwin,[3] in a long and abstruse passage but with some justice, attributed the growth of this view to the prevailing allegiance to the Spencerian form of Darwinian biology, which made the law put forth "organs of accommodation" with the environment. Corwin was only repeating in a longer and more elegant form Mr. Dooley's tart observation that "the Supreme Court follows the election returns."

John R. Schmidhauser[4] carefully analyzed the effects that the backgrounds and personalities of the justices played in the historic role of the Supreme Court and drew some striking conclusions, especially applicable to the last generation. He warned that evaluation of individual justices depends largely on whether one approves of their ideologies, but that if the data is treated with sensitivity, it permits certain tentative conclusions. For one thing, not all the "great" judges were true jurisprudents but, like John Marshall, depended on others for their legal philosophy.

Schmidhauser's examination is far more extensive, but in summary it reinforces an observation made in 1717 by Benjamin Hoadly, Bishop of Bangor: "Whosoever hath an absolute authority to interpret any written or spoken laws, it is he who is truly the lawgiver, to all intents and purposes, and not the person who first wrote or spoke them."

---

[2] *Life Magazine,* August, 1935. Reprinted by permission.

[3] Edward S. Corwin, *Court over Constitution: A Study of Judicial Review as an Instrument of Popular Government* (Princeton University Press, 1938), pages 125-127.

[4] *The Supreme Court: Its Politics, Personalities, and Procedures* (New York: Holt, Rinehart and Winston, 1960), pages 154-157.

It seems to me that during the 1950's and 1960's the Supreme Court was all too often assuming the power to keep the people from doing wrong—that is, wrong as defined by the fallible justices. I am aware, of course, that the Warren Court often stepped in where the political angels of Congress feared to tread and began the institution of some much-needed reforms. But circumstances changed with such lightning rapidity in the 1960's that one vacillates between the emotions of the heart and the dictates of the mind. This will explain why, as will be seen later, I seek to enlarge the Supreme Court, to refresh its membership continuously and considerably, and to make its decisions subject to the popular changes reflected in this refreshment.

In examining the historic role of the Supreme Court, one cannot overlook the legal realists, of whom Justice Holmes was the supreme example. It is true that Holmes was a Social Darwinist in the hardest sense of the term, and believed that change was the sole law of the universe; yet he could write that "The first requirement of a sound body of law is, that it should correspond with the actual feelings and demands of the community, whether right or wrong." This was much the same as the dictum of Solon, uttered twenty-five centuries before and referred to previously. When the critics remonstrated that he could have written a much better code of laws for Athens than he had, he answered, "The lawgiver should attempt no more good than the people can bear."

Holmes held that the laws should be interpreted broadly, that the courts should assume that the legislators really represented the opinion of the community. This was the ground taken in later years by Justice Frankfurter in his opposition to many of the decisions of the "Warren Court." Holmes has been remembered mostly for his dissenting opinions eventually approved by the Court.

The doctrine that judges create the law was expanded by Judge Jerome Frank in his argument that the law is not immutable but is made by courts as well as legislators. In fact, said he, most judges had come to agree with an ignorant public that there is a "law of nature," and that law is "found" rather than "created." Frank found certain psychological reasons for this belief and pled for that emotional maturity without which we cannot recognize that man is not made for the law, but that the law is made by and for man.

There is now, perhaps unfortunately, little challenge of the Supreme Court's self-assumed role as guardian of the Constitution, though there is, and always has been, a great deal of criticism about the way it performs the function. There have been complaints that the justices are chosen for their politics or their ideologies. It is variously said that their life tenure assures that they will be unresponsive to changing times or that they become too responsive because they cannot be reined in by constituents. They are criticized in one breath for hewing too closely to the line of the Constitution and ignoring its spirit and in the next for not hewing closely enough. The bitterest attacks in recent years have focused on—among other things—what are interpreted as the Court's tendencies (1) to judge by "sociological" rather than Constitutional principles, and (2) to give the criminal all the advantages in its laudable but "misguided" attempts to shield the innocent.

Without presuming to weigh the validity of these criticisms, one must recognize that if the Court is actually seeking to set things right with moral trends, this has some resemblance to the current rage for "presentism" among historians and social scientists. And this, in turn, as has been pointed out by the Constitutional historian Alfred H. Kelly, is "a Marxist-type perversion of the relation between truth and utility." The assumption in many quarters today is that history and economics can be rewritten to serve the interests of one's own ideology, whether libertarian, conservative, or totalitarian.

In every generation critics of the Court have accused it of reading its desired meanings into the Constitution, and the charge is proven by the way in which successive Courts have passed down directly contradictory opinions. We may as well reconcile ourselves to the plain fact that the justices are human beings who will never be able to rid themselves of all the effects of the subtle influences that operate on human beings.[5]

THE POWERS OF THE SENATE

Perhaps we can change the conditions under which justices are appointed and under which they operate, even while recognizing that they can never hope to please everybody. My proposal for reconstitution of the Senate is based on the historical fact that Parliament, though not composed exclusively of lawyers, was originally England's High Court, and my present conviction that, by the revival of that usage, we can provide our system of government with a much-needed balance wheel. In short, the Senate should become a truly deliberative body—a combination of courts of last resort, grand jury, censor, and ombudsman.

As was proposed in Chapter 3, Congress, with the consent of the Senate, should have the power to define all forms of civil and criminal offenses, though the power might be yielded to the States for a limited time. Hopefully, this would do much to reform the present definition of misdemeanors—simple drunkenness, drug addiction, and many charges and counter-charges in divorce cases. The proposed system frankly copies that of Canada, and moreover, as in Canada, original jurisdiction in Federal cases would lie with State Courts.

Appeals could be made in Federal cases to Federal circuit courts, and certain categories of cases would be tried in special Federal courts—Claims, Customs, Internal Revenue, Patents, Military Appeals, Admiralty, and the like. True, State courts are at present years behind in hearing cases, but this situation is by no

---

[5]Further valuable references to the role of the courts are Henry Steele Commager, *Majority Rule and Minority Rights* (New York: Oxford, 1943); Charles Black, *The People and the Court: Judicial Review in a Democracy* (New York: Macmillan, 1960); Roscoe Pound, *The Spirit of the Common Law* (Boston: Marshall Jones, 1921); Jerome Frank, *Law and the Modern Mind* (New York: Brentano, 1930); and Edward M. Burns, *Ideas in Conflict* (New York: Norton, 1960).

means inevitable. My proposal is that, as the States are consolidated, they include judicial reform in their new constitutions and greatly enlarge the number of their courts and organize a Judicial Assembly.

It is quite possible that the nature and functions of this Senate would not attract those extroverts, even among lawyers, whose tastes and ambitions point them toward the political forum. This is as it should be, for they would be more useful in Congress. Since the membership of the Senate would be continually changing as Senators died or reached the age of retirement, this would mean that the membership of the Senate's courts and commissions would be in continual process of refreshment. But within these limits the Senate would be self-regulating. It would elect its presiding officer, the Chief Justice, and he would appoint its courts and commissions with the consent of the body. Moreover, as Chief of State, he would not only serve as the symbol of justice, the highest aim of the nation, but would act as the ceremonial head and, whenever there was an interim between Presidents, as the executive.

The Senate would exercise certain checks on Congress. It would lay out the Congressional districts after each census, set the guidelines for political campaigns, and be the judge of elections. Its consent would be necessary to create or alter the boundaries of States and to create or continue regulatory agencies. It would share with Congress the right to enforce uniform guidelines for the States' administration of certain of their powers. It would impeach or remove judges, and would supervise lower courts, as the Supreme Court does today. It could and, it is to be hoped, would insist that the processes of the courts be simplified and speeded up.

It could suspend Congressional legislation for six months. It could recommend legislation to Congress and demand that it be voted up or down, and if Congress in three successive years rejected it or failed to act satisfactorily, the Senate by a two-thirds vote could dissolve Congress and call for new elections, which naturally would be a plebiscite on that issue. It could propose amendments to the Constitution, see that they were adequately publicized, and then submit them to popular vote. The public would need a long period of education before it would accept some vitally needed changes, and in my opinion the Senate must be in a position to undertake this.

There are many matters which a politically oriented Congress will not touch, or at best will skirt with cautious and sometimes meaningless compromises; even then it often emasculates a law by refusing to appropriate money for its enforcement. We can mention, almost off-hand, nearly a score of subjects on which it temporizes: effectively socialized medicine; a guaranteed standard of living; adequate airports and fair treatment of air controllers; an arrogant Pentagon wastefully spending huge sums for unneeded armaments; speeding up justice by reform of antiquated legal processes, including the wasteful and often unnecessary and even unjust jury system; redefining minor crimes and their treatment and at the same time going after organized crime more seriously than the overrated Mr. J. Edgar Hoover ever did; reform of prisons and the parole system; higher standards and more adequate inducements for law enforcement officers; reform of our insurance companies and banks, which often fall so far short of fulfilling their functions that they are little better than parasites; heedless waste of resources in over-production and planned obsolescence; over-population; pollution of the environment; safety standards not only for roads, vehicles, and mines, but for nearly everything else; drug addiction; racism; schools; protection of consumers; civil rights; food and drug standards; the balancing of social costs against industrial and economic practices. Finally, there is the problem of how to prepare the country to spend its growing leisure time in ways that are personally and socially fruitful—or at least not boring or destructive. One thing that might be done is to draft the nation's youth for non-military services in conservation projects, social work as medical and hospital aides, assistant teachers, etc., etc.[6]

Now of course these problems cannot be solved all of a sudden, nor could the new Senate legislate their solutions. But the Senate would have the means to keep them in the public eye and to demand that Congress act or run the risk of an unpleasant national plebiscite. The Constitutional injunction on the Senate to make studies and investigations would force it to search for spreading social cancers and also to serve as an early warning tocsin of coming changes that government and society must prepare to meet. But perhaps even more important to the rule of justice would be the duty of the Senate to set up courts or panels that would act as ombudsmen to protect the rights of citizens.

The Senate would also set up from among its Law Senators certain courts of last resort. Such courts would deal with specific types of cases on final appeal, but matters of Constitutional interpretation would be decided by the entire body. This system would have the advantage of distributing (and, hopefully, reducing) the Supreme Court's present burden of cases and would allow more time for reflection, something that is all but universally regarded as a present lack. Moreover, the justices would be able to sound out among their colleagues a far wider range of knowledge and experience than could be found among the present nine Platonic guardians.

An added judicial function would be the power of the Senate in times of public disaster or peril from crime, subversion, war, or other causes to suspend the writ of habeas corpus, authorize summary searches and seizures, or declare martial law, applicable to all or any part of the country—but with appeals in cases of abuse available by law as provided by the Senate. The long dispute over Lincoln's right to suspend habeas corpus should be a warning to us, for in this day and age there will be crises which cannot be handled by the ordinary processes of the

---

[6]Publishers' lists are filled with books bearing on these and related subjects. Among many we might mention Alexander M. Bickel, *The Supreme Court and the Idea of Progress* (New York: Harper and Row, 1970); Richard Harris, *Justice: The Crisis of Law, Order, and Freedom in America* (New York: Dutton, 1970); John P. Frank, *American Law: The Case for Radical Reform* (New York: Macmillan, 1970); Philip B. Kurland, ed., *The Supreme Court and the Constitution* (University of Chicago Press, 1965).

courts. After all is said and done in the line of political theory, the fact remains that there will be crises when government must be substantively unchecked if it is to be effective.

THE ROLE OF THE CHIEF JUSTICE

I have not emphasized the role of the Chief Justice in defining the powers of the Senate, but he would obviously be the key officer of the body. Elected from among the Senators, serving for only five years, and charged (with the consent of the Senate) with appointing deputies, members of the courts of last resort, and all committees and commissions, he would be a man of power, but with both power and tenure limited. Since he could not exercise executive power for more than brief periods—if at all—there is no danger that he would become a Caesar. The intention is to avoid making one man a permanent judicial fixture and arbiter lest he make the Senate so inflexible that it would stand in the way of reasoned change and thus thwart the very purpose for which it was reconstituted.

As ceremonial head of the nation he would assume many of the onerous but more or less meaningless functions that now devolve on the President, perhaps living in the White House, historically the ceremonial headquarters of the nation. Indeed, it would be better that way, for it would aid in reducing the awesomeness of the Presidency, which has made the official in that office so dictatorial and remote.

On the other hand, perhaps there ought to be a certain remoteness about the Chief Justice, for he would be above all else a judge and censor, the personification and fountain of national justice. Rightly conducted, his office would not be a puck in the political game, as the Presidency is. Though the Senate would have a definite share in the nation's business, and inevitably its actions would at times be controversial, yet it would occupy a loftier place than the Congress, and presumably its pronouncements and demands would be made only after careful study and would receive a more respectful hearing by the public than the political actions of President and Congress.

Moreover, the Chief Justice and the Senate ordinarily could and probably would operate quietly, and would spurn lobbyists, as the present Supreme Court presumably does. Its panels of ombudsmen throughout the nation would not only listen to complainants and follow through on cases to see that justice is done, but would keep the Senate informed of areas in which reforms are needed but which a politically oriented Congress will not touch. And the recommendation after long and careful study of a reform bill to Congress should not only bring public pressure to bear on that body but should relieve it of some of the political pressures against the legislation.

Finally, the Chief Justice and the Senate would be the guarantors that the electoral processes are as fair as possible and are being properly observed. Thus they would preserve democracy while at the same time in the capacities of judges and censors preventing hasty and ill-considered political action and keeping watch against the possibility of tyranny by the majority.

THE SENATE AND THE FUTURE

It is clear that the Senate would have to be quite different from what it is now or ever has been, for its functions (whether juristic or not) would require men and women with judicious rather than political minds—much as Supreme Court justices ought to be; in fact, they would be the Supreme Court. But they ought also to be realists, unhampered by ideological chains or value judgments insofar as that is humanly possible, and well aware that problems cannot be solved by merely taking thought or, conversely, by overthrowing existing institutions without taking responsibility for adequate substitutes. Of course, the Senate, as I envision it, would include thoughtful advocates of tradition who can distinguish between the good and the bad in the new.

The fundamental struggle of our time is between the old economy of scarcity and the new and as yet amorphous economy of abundance. America and Western Europe are being torn between the two, and presumably the struggle will eventually spread to many parts of the "developing" world. Society is apparently being polarized, in the usual view between revolution and reaction. Yet one might question this. Perhaps the real struggle is between the poor and the comfortable, and the design of the so-called revolutionists is merely to hasten the coming of the economy of abundance and spread the comfort more widely.

Change is on the way, and the "retooling and redirection" of our society in the coming generation—that is, before the year 2000—is a task of such complexity as well as world-shaking consequences that it is safe to say that not one American adult in fifty has grasped it. The near future obviously holds dangers to human existence and the environment from waste of resources, over-population, pollution, and nuclear radioactivity, not to mention world-wide holocaust. Even more alarming are the scientific, chiefly biological, discoveries that are even now taking place.[7]

---

[7]Journalists examine them from time to time, but there are a number of convenient summaries. Robert W. Prehoda, *Designing the Future: The Role of Technological Forecasting* (Philadelphia: Chilton Book Co., 1967) examines economic, mechanical, and biological progress and possibilities, and appends a useful bibliography. *Profiles of the Future: An Inquiry into the Limits of the Possible* (New York: Harper and Row, 1962), is by Arthur C. Clarke, not only a science-fictioneer but a highly respected scientist who first proposed the communications satellites that now hover above Earth. Gordon Rattray Taylor's *The Biological Time Bomb* (New York: World Publishing Co., 1968) may be alarmist but it "gives one to think," and his *Doomsday Book* (New York: World Publishing Co., 1970) goes into the problem of whether mankind is committing suicide.

During recent generations human knowledge has increased by geometric progression. It was only fifty years from Roentgen's X rays to the atomic bomb, and from Goddard's mathematical equations in the 1920's it was less than half a century until Neil Armstrong stepped on the surface of the moon. Now we face not merely possibilities but certainties that will change the world beyond all recognition—if it survives.

Biological wonders have already become common, and new wonders are just over the horizon. The "green revolution" promises to increase the output of agriculture manyfold and in countries like India has not only already bred rebellion among traditionalists but is breaking down the distribution system. But biologists are going ruthlessly on with their experiments, whether for good or evil. They have pierced to the basic elements of life and actually catalyzed amino acids in the laboratory, constructed the enzyme ribonuclease, and synthesized a gene. Parthenogenesis has long since been induced in sea urchins and frogs—that is, the eggs can be made to germinate without the aid of male sperm. Vegetables have been cloned by the division of a single cell into vast numbers of genetically identical cells, and the process will undoubtedly be applied to animals. Just ahead is the certainty that genes and sex can be controlled, and the probability that there will be the test-tube babies foretold by Aldous Huxley in *Brave New World* (1932). The process of aging has been slowed down—or at least life has been prolonged. Infants now being born may actually have a life expectancy of a century, and their children may live for centuries—what a dreary prospect! Scientists are now working on ways to control social characteristics, moods, memory, and intelligence by genetic or chemical means—even to the curing of insanity. It may even be possible to wage genetic warfare.

It is a common belief that computers can only memorize and compute on the basis of what is fed to them—that, in other words, they are and always will be incapable of thought. Nevertheless, even today they play chess, compose music, translate from one language to another, design other computers, learn from experience and profit from their mistakes, show a certain inquisitiveness about their surroundings, and exhibit a phenomenon strangely analogous to human "nervous breakdowns." Even now there is a computer able to encompass all human knowledge in a six-foot cube. True, such computers will not be able to do anything human beings could not do, given time, but with their superior capacity and lightning speed they may "escape from our control by sheer speed of operation."[8] But even beyond that looms the possibility of linking a computer with a human brain (disembodied or not), producing a "cyborg," a thing capable of thought at a level beyond present comprehension.

Communications satellites, now in their infancy, will make it possible to dial persons anywhere in the world and see and talk to them. Electric power will be

[8]A. C. Clarke, *Profiles of the Future,* page 215.

manufactured by the rays of the sun, by the tides, by steam escaping from volcanic vents, or by nuclear means free from irradiation and probably almost self-renewing—and may even be transmitted without wires. We can, if we will, produce pollution-free means of smelting metals and powering automobiles; or at least we can stop the razing of the green fields and trees on which we depend for the renewal of our oxygen supply. These tasks should have priority over space exploration, though in the end we may be able to transport needed metals from the moon or the tiny asteroids so plentiful in space.

In the light of all these changes, the attention I have given to our judicial system seems so paltry as to constitute not even a palliative to our problem. If, for example, we solved the problems of crime by medicating the water supply, we probably would also destroy the reasoned dissent on which our system of democracy depends for continual refreshment. The future may fulfill the brightest dreams of the Utopians—or it may outdo the most monstrous imaginings of science fictioneers. In either case, it would clearly be a future that our present institutions are not equipped to meet—a time when the dizzying pace of the past three decades will in retrospect seem an era of peace and quiet.

There was a time not many generations ago when scientists were looked on as necromancers, warlocks, and consorts of the devil, and were shunned and persecuted accordingly. Friar Roger Bacon, the inventor of gunpowder, died in prison as a sorcerer, and Giordano Bruno was burned at the stake. Then with the Enlightenment the popular mind began to veer, and by the end of the last century scientists were so rapidly furnishing the means to raise the standard of living that they were being hailed as the saviors of the world. The atomic bomb introduced a shock of doubt, and this doubt is rapidly taking the shape of an anti-scientific movement. The social changes that will occur are simply beyond our power to grasp. Already there is a cry that medical and hospital costs are so high that not even the middle class can afford them, and that medical marvels—for example, kidney dialysis machines—are not being made available rapidly enough.

What will happen when the biological time bomb bursts with all its promises and horrors? Will it be possible to endow every child with genius and to expand every man's life indefinitely? What of those who cannot share these doubtful "blessings"? What if it becomes advisable to put the hopelessly idiotic or deformed to eternal sleep, or to sterilize persons who carry hereditary diseases such as hemophilia or Huntington's chorea, or anyone who has the "47, XYY chromosome" now being blamed (whether or not correctly) for criminal tendencies in the possessor? Who shall be allowed to procreate; eventually will anyone be allowed to bring up a family in the traditional manner? And what of the problems of morality—not to mention bigotry—involved? And of the nations that do not share in the new science? And of the deadly viruses that escape from the laboratories and spread death and destruction?

The social and moral disorientations and frustrations, even should people happen to dwell in the midst of material affluence, may well become so unbearable. It is easy to imagine the masses all over the world revolting against scientists, the suppression of the masses by genocide on a scale Hitler and Stalin never dreamed of, and the emergence of an élite class exercising undisputed ascendance over a docile population of de-sexed, robot-like humans, subservient chimeras, and oh, yes—cyborgs, half animal or human, half machines.

How can humanity—we in a democracy—hope to cope with such problems when we won't even look far enough ahead to educate the medical practitioners of whom the country is in dire need? We pour our substance into useless production for wars that yield nothing but power and profits for the favored few, deprive a fifth of our society of more than a bare subsistence, and hang on to the artificial prejudices that forbid the acceptance as a brother of a man with a dark skin or a different religion or culture. This is not an indictment solely of the United States, but of humanity everywhere.

In 1896 William Jennings Bryan went about the country trumpeting that "the people have a right to make their own mistakes." And so they have! But that does not mean we should abandon Jefferson's injunction that "if we think [the people] . . . not enlightened enough to exercise their control with a wholesome discretion, the remedy is not to take it from them, but to inform their discretion by education." A government based on political rivalry, however democratic and formalized the struggle may be, is not equipped to prepare for such a future. That is why I propose a Senate that hopefully can act not merely as a court, but even more importantly as investigator, censor, and above all as educator.

Chapter 9

RETURN TO PHILADELPHIA

Throughout this volume I have sought to make it clear that what I have in mind is flexibility. Probably the Founding Fathers did not have this in mind in Philadelphia, though we have done them all but irreparable injustice in assuming that they thought they had wrought for all time. Alexander Hamilton wrote privately that the Constitution was "a frail and worthless fabric"—then set himself in *The Federalist* to give it lasting shape and value. In 1816 Jefferson wrote to his friend Samuel Kercheval:

> Some men look at constitutions with sanctimonious reverence, and deem them like the ark of the covenant, too sacred to be touched. They ascribe to the men of the preceding age a wisdom more than human, and suppose what they did to be beyond amendment. I knew that age well; I belonged to it, and labored with it. It deserved well of its country. It was very like the present, but without the experience of the present; and forty years of experience in government is worth a century of book-reading; and this they would say themselves, were they to rise from the dead. I am certainly not an advocate for frequent and untried changes in laws and constitutions. I think moderate imperfections had better be borne with; because, when once known, we accommodate ourselves to them, and find practical means of correcting their ill effects. But I know also, that laws and institutions must go hand in hand with the progress of the human mind. As that becomes more developed, more enlightened, as new discoveries are made, new truths disclosed, and manners and opinions change with the change of circum-

stances, institutions must advance also, and keep pace with the times. We might as well require a man to wear still the coat which fitted him when a boy, as civilized society to remain ever under the regimen of their barbarous ancestors.

We could go on quoting the opinions of reasonable men about the Constitution, such as Woodrow Wilson's comment that it "was not meant to hold the government back to the time of horses and wagons." But the greatest statement of all is doubtless that by Justice Holmes in his dissenting opinion in *Abrams v. U.S.* (1919):

> When men have realized that time has upset many fighting faiths, they may come to believe even more than they believe the very foundations of their own conduct that the ultimate good desired is better reached by free trade in ideas —that the best test of truth is the power of the thought to get itself accepted in the competition of the market, and that truth is the only ground upon which their wishes safely can be carried out. That, at any rate, is the theory of our Constitution. It is an experiment, as all life is an experiment. Every year if not every day we have to wager our salvation upon some prophecy based upon imperfect knowledge. While that experiment is part of our system I think that we should be eternally vigilant against attempts to check the expression of opinions that we loathe and believe to be fraught with death, unless they so imminently threaten immediate interference with the lawful and pressing purposes of the law that an immediate check is required to save the country.

Have we reached the time when an immediate check is required to save the country? In my opinion we have. I do not mean that our government is in serious danger of being overthrown by armed revolution from within, but I do believe that the processes of justice have become so paralyzed that we may even come to welcome the traditional "man on horseback." Granted, much of the dissent we see and hear is merely moral posturing by youngsters—illiterate despite their university degrees—who know little or nothing about the true nature of democracy and in their impatience refuse to read and absorb the lessons of its slow evolution.

But there is something wrong when even a small part of a youthful generation denounce American ideals as hypocritical and spit upon the flag as the symbol of oppression. There is something wrong when even a few resort to bombing, in imitation of the nihilists who around the turn of the century murdered six heads of state. That the canker permeates more than idealistic youth is shown by the fact that in barely five years six prominent Americans were shot down: the Kennedy brothers, Malcolm X, Medgar Evans, Martin Luther King, and George Lincoln Rockwell. Who will be next? There is even a curious bit of evidence, albeit wryly reversed, in the incredible report that the Mafia openly picketed an FBI office as unfair to organized crime!

One can cite many viewings with alarm among political scientists, but it is the rare observer who will boldly pierce to the roots of the problems in the Constitution itself and advocate basic change.[1] Indeed, many political scientists warn that mechanical tinkering with the Constitution will solve nothing—it is the "men" that count—and say quite frankly that the present system is so deeply imbedded in the hearts and minds of the people and so deeply entrenched in the self-interest of Congressmen and their States that it cannot be changed; we have an atavistic fear of strong leadership and distrust of clear-cut programs. Those who wish change, says David B. Truman, "lack more than a toe hold on reality." Some see a faint hope that Congress will change itself, while others are resigned to wait for a change in the political environment. Perhaps they are right. Perhaps the time is not yet ripe for party or Constitutional change, and eventually we may have to go through a period of ideological conflict and then the advent of a Caesar.

The American Political Science Association's *Toward a More Responsible Two-Party System* (1950) was mentioned in Chapter 6. The committee which made the report ended its analysis and recommendations on a note that shows an almost eerie foresight in its exposition of the dangers bound to follow "inaction in the face of needed change." Read this:

> Four of these dangers warrant special emphasis. The first danger is that the inadequacy of the party system in sustaining well-considered programs and providing broad public support for them may lead to grave consequences in an explosive era. The second danger is that the American people may go too far for the safety of constitutional government in compensating for this inadequacy by shifting excessive responsibility to the President. The third danger is that with growing public cynicism and continuing proof of the ineffectiveness of the party system the nation may eventually witness the disintegration of the two major parties. The fourth danger is that the incapacity of the two parties for consistent action based on meaningful programs may rally support for extremist parties poles apart, each fanatically bent on imposing on the country its particular panacea.[2]

Even that long ago the committee was aware of the growing number of ideological activists who might succeed in destroying the American system of political tension and compromise which, however clumsy and inefficient, had worked thus far save for the disastrous split in 1860. The problem is far greater today with

---

[1]Among the few exceptions are William MacDonald, *A New Constitution for a New America* (1921); W. Y. Elliott, *The Need for Constitutional Reform* (1935); Henry Hazlitt, *A New Constitution Now* (1942); and R. G. Tugwell, *Model for a New Constitution* (Santa Barbara: The Center for the Study of Democratic Institutions, 1970).

[2]Report on Committee on Political Parties, in the *Supplement* to *The American Political Science Review,* xliv, no. 3, part 2 (Sept. 1950), page 92.

the multiplication of ideological activists who, if they can ever agree among themselves on two opposing stands, may force polarization on the political parties. Ideological polarization, of course, would strengthen party loyalty and activism, but it might also lead eventually to civil war. It is remarkable that, even though about to be ridden down by those four Apocalyptic horsemen, the committee could suggest no more effective protection than a barricade of reeds intended to shore up the party system.

I used the dread term "civil war" above because I cannot find anywhere in our present set-up any reliable means of forestalling it permanently. Certainly we cannot rely on an army or a national guard many of whose conscripts agree with civil dissidents black or white—two quite possibly antagonistic elements. Indeed, the army and national guard are already showing evidences of rebellion against government policy, including attempts to impose domestic law and order.

It is readily apparent that political scientists and Constitutional thinkers in general stand paralyzed before the basilisk of feasibility. I suspect that one objection to calling a Constitutional convention is that it would open the way for an ideological battle that might rend the country asunder—would at the very least further embitter political relations. Anything proposed would be disruptive. These fears may be well based, but the alternative is worse. It reminds one of Maurice Chevalier's *mot:* when someone asked him how he liked being old he replied that in the face of the alternative he found it quite satisfactory.

If it is true, as I believe, that we are facing a moral revolution, it would still be unwise, even if we could agree on the definition of that new morality, to write it into the Constitution. Morals change; we should not overlook the shameful fact that slavery was written into the Constitution of 1787. A more recent example was Douglas MacArthur's insistence that the Japanese Constitution renounce war. But mistakes can be made in realms other than the moral. It is apparent that our Faustian drive to create and produce must be moderated—greatly and soon —or we will not only destroy our environment but irretrievably ruin the physical bases upon which our freedom has been built. But none of this can be written into the Constitution; it must be born in the hearts and minds of the citizenry.

Perhaps it will mean some limitations of the freedoms we have enjoyed during what we have hitherto regarded as time's anteroom to Utopia. Who shall be permitted to own a car? Who shall pay for cleaning up the polluted environment? Who shall be permitted to reproduce, and how many children may they have? These are real questions, not for the future but now. We are becoming painfully aware that a few hundred explosives and bacteriological experts could literally put our government and our technical civilization out of business in one night, and possibly keep it out. A problem like overpopulation will be solved sooner or later—by wars and epidemics if not by rational means. Many aspects of Puritanism must and will pass away, but our culture will be destroyed unless we keep intact that central Puritan concept, stated by Ralph Barton Perry, that "requires the forging of a will which is stronger than any natural appetite."

Life styles inevitably change, and they should, but the warping effects of sex without responsibility and of love romanticized beyond all reason, not to mention racism, drugs, and crime, can destroy the very foundations of society. So also can the mushrooming of nationalism in the "developing" nations and the debilitating struggles between bigoted ideologies, whether economic, political, or philosophical formulas. All of these things—and others not named here, or perhaps not yet known—face us with endless frightening prospects: the poisoning of food crops, the gelatinization of the oceans, rivalry in space, biological warfare, and nuclear holocaust. More and more we begin to doubt Bodin's idea of progress, which has been our guiding light for four centuries, and wonder if it is not a mere will-o'-the-wisp. Perhaps the Oriental doctrine of the wheel is true after all.

Now of course few if any of these problems can be settled by legislative fiat, but they do require deep inquiry, a reasonable spirit, and a corps of leaders and thinkers who are little short of being inspired prophets. And even if, through some series of miracles, we should solve them for ourselves, what of the rest of the world? The decisions cannot be left, as hitherto, to a runaway democracy that bases its decisions on selfish local interests and religious, economic, and race prejudices; and most certainly not to a profit motive which we now know has made hash of Adam Smith's doctrine that the "invisible hand" of a market economy will automatically and eternally promote the greatest good of society. These are the reasons why I have sought to suggest ways in which democracy can be linked with a greater degree of rational oversight, not only of the processes of government but of the rights of the citizen.

However all that may be, the Legislative Reference Service noted (October 1970) that thirty-three States have petitioned Congress to call a Constitutional convention. True enough, two requests have lapsed because of a seven-year limitation, three have been withdrawn, and one was invalidated by a Federal court. Nevertheless, though the Constitution of 1787 does not specifically state that Congress can call a Constitutional convention on its own volition, William MacDonald was probably justified in suggesting that Congress has the right. It may be that the men behind this legislative call were seeking primarily to cancel out certain decisions of the Supreme Court—such as "one man, one vote," or the desegregation of schools—but we may soon have to face the perils of a convention, like it or not, and it is time we begin to think about the kind of Constitution we want. Probably the most realistic approach would be for professional and legal organizations to advance their proposals for Constitutional reform and bring pressure on Congress and the States to launch them either as amendments or to call a Constitutional convention.

The historian might well ask what would have happened to the new-born nation if the young men who met in Philadelphia in the spring and summer of 1787 had acknowledged that their task was not only impossible but that if they completed it there was no chance it would be adopted. It is this very paralysis that at first moved me to put the word "impertinent" into the title of this volume, for I had been assured that not only were my proposals not pertinent to the times but that they impertinently challenged the old and well tried. But then I recalled the words spoken by Washington in opening the Constitutional Convention:

> It is too probable that no plan we propose will be adopted. Perhaps another dreadful conflict is to be sustained. If to please the people we offer what we ourselves disapprove, how can we afterward defend our work? Let us raise a standard to which the wise and honest can repair. The rest is in the hand of God.

A REVISED CONSTITUTION OF THE UNITED STATES

CONTENTS

PREAMBLE

We the people of the United States, acting as sources and final arbiters of the laws, in order to form a more perfect union, establish justice, insure domestic tranquility, provide for the common defense, promote the general welfare, and secure the blessings of liberty to ourselves and our posterity, do ordain and establish this Constitution for the United States of America. The government of the United

States shall be vested in a Congress, and in a judiciary headed by a Senate, and such officials as they Constitutionally select or provide for. These shall be, among others, a Chief Justice of the United States who serves as Chief of State under the oversight of the Senate, and a President who acts as the executive arm of the Congress under the legislative oversight of the Congress and the judicial and investigatory oversight of the Senate. This Constitution and the laws of the United States that shall be made in pursuance thereof; and all treaties made, or that shall be made, under the authority of the United States, shall be the supreme law of the land; and the judges in every State shall be bound thereby, anything in the constitution or laws of any State to the contrary notwithstanding. Nothing in this Constitution shall be interpreted as invalidating guarantees and safeguards to persons as hitherto established by the Constitution of 1787, the Congress, and the Courts, save as provided herein.

ARTICLE I.   THE CONGRESS

Section 1. *A Unicameral Legislature.*   With such exceptions as are stated hereafter the powers formerly granted to the Senate and the House of Representatives are henceforth lodged in the one House of Congress with 200 elected members, who shall serve five-year terms unless sooner dissolved. The Congress shall continue to be numbered as before, with a new Congress assuming office after each election.

Section 2. *Fiscal Powers of Congress.*   (1) Congress shall have the power to borrow money; to lay and collect taxes, including graduated income taxes; and to lay duties, imposts, and excises. It shall have the sole right to regulate persons or corporations engaged in interstate or foreign trade; to make laws concerning bankruptcies; and to coin money and issue currency and to punish counterfeiting thereof.

(2) Congress at its discretion may assume the sole power to acquire, and/or to approve the acquisition by others, and to regulate the establishment and administration of banks and all other fiscal institutions and media, including those engaged in insurance, in futures, or in issuing or dealing in stocks, bonds, and other securities.

(3) No money shall be drawn from the treasury, but in consequence of appropriations made by law; and a regular statement and account of the receipts and expenditures of all public money shall be published from time to time. But though Congress may undertake obligations extending over a greater period, it shall fix and pass its ordinary budget every two years, after which no appropriation shall be lowered or withheld save by a two-thirds vote of the full body, including Congressmen-at-Large and Congressmen-pro-Forma, officials who are hereafter defined.

Section 3. *Powers to Regulate Industry, Commerce, Communications, and Natural Resources.* (1) Congress shall have the sole power to regulate the exploitation of all lake and ocean fisheries and of ocean resources to the limits of the continental shelf or such other limits as it shall set; to regulate all commerce with foreign nations and among the several States; to regulate conditions on Indian reservations; to establish postal services and to arrange with foreign nations for handling mails and other means of transportation and communication; to regulate the navigation of rivers, lakes, and coastal waters, and all means of interstate traffic and communication; and to regulate any engagement by its citizens in space exploration, colonization, or communication.

(2) Congress shall have the sole right to grant patents and copyrights for a limited time and to arrange with other nations for similar privileges. It shall also have the sole power to define weights and measures, and shall provide for the general adoption of the metric system within a definite period of time, making only such exceptions as are necessitated by irrevocable actions such as the survey of the public domain.

(3) Congress shall have the sole power to pass laws regulating immigration and naturalization of foreigners; and upon just cause being shown before the courts, immigrants may be expelled and/or naturalization rescinded.

Section 4. *Power to Define Crimes.* (1) Congress, with the consent of the Senate, shall have the power to define all forms of civil and criminal offenses, to control the manufacture, distribution, and ownership of weapons, and to set penalties, applicable in both Federal and State Courts. With the consent of the Senate and in exceptional cases, Congress may by law place these powers, or some of them, in the hands of the States, but for no more than five years at a time.

(2) Treason against the United States shall consist only in levying war against it, or in adhering to its enemies, giving them aid and comfort. No person shall be convicted of treason unless on the testimony of two witnesses to the same overt act, or on confession in open court. The Senate shall have power to declare the punishment of treason, but no attainder of treason shall entail corruption of blood or forfeiture except during the life of the person attainted.

Section 5. *War Powers.* Congress shall have the sole right to make war, except that in case of attack the President may act to protect the country, nor shall any public or private military personnel, matériel, or financial support be supplied to foreign nations without the specific consent of Congress. Congress shall have the sole right to make rules concerning captures and to define and punish piracies and felonies on the high seas, in the air, and in space, and offenses against the law of nations. It shall have the sole right to raise and support armed forces and make rules for their governance, and provide for the raising of militia forces in the States, their maintenance, training, and inspection, and make rules for their governance and for calling them into active service by Federal or State governments. No soldier shall be quartered in any house in time of peace without the consent of the owner, nor in time of war but in a manner to be prescribed by law.

Section 6. *Powers over the Public Domain and Public Property.* Congress shall exercise eminent domain and dispose of and make all needful rules and regulations respecting the territory or other property belonging to the United States save that falling within the control of the Senate.

Section 7. *Special Powers of Legislation.* Congress shall have the sole power, with the consent of two-thirds of the Senate, to legislate on human procreation, sterilization, suicide, euthanasia, and on useful and/or novel biological and medical experimentation and practices.

Section 8. *Duties Toward and Aid to the States.* (1) Congress may admit new states to the Union, but no new State shall be formed or erected within the jurisdiction of any other State, nor any State be formed by the junction of two or more States or parts of States, nor any territory transferred from one State to another without the consent of two-thirds of the Senate.

(2) To aid the States in carrying out their functions, Congress may by uniform legislation grant them certain proportions of Federal tax receipts, or control of certain forms of taxation normally controlled by Congress; however such expenditures and controls shall be subject to inspection by Congress and Senate and may in the case of any State be rescinded by Congress with the approval of a simple majority.

(3) Congress shall guarantee to every State in this Union a republican form of government, and shall protect each of them against attack and domestic violence.

Section 9. *Conditional Powers of Congress.* (1) In addition to the foregoing powers Congress may exercise certain powers which otherwise would accrue to the States. In such instances regulations may establish uniform guidelines, inspection and, in case of need, financing, but their intrastate administration shall be in the hands of the States. However, when the Senate declares that a State is not carrying out the law in a satisfactory manner, the Congress, by a two-thirds majority and with the consent of the Senate, may impose Federal administration for a period of five years, and this period may be extended for five years; but it may not be permanently imposed except by Constitutional amendment. Notwithstanding, in case a State refuses to abide by Congressional guidelines, Congress may refuse to grant the State any financial or technical aid to be used in the exercise of the power in question.

(2) Under these conditions Congress may:

Establish uniform regulations for marriage and divorce and financial arrangements pertaining to them, legitimize births, and make laws concerned with inheritance, testaments, and the transfer of property among relatives by blood or marriage.

Provide for public housing, and provide housing and/or maintenance for the unemployed, the indigent, dependent children, and aged and handicapped persons.

Establish regulations for the teaching and practice of medicine and its branches, and regulate hospitals, asylums, sanitariums, convalescent and nursing homes, homes for children, the aged, and the handicapped, and other such institutions.

Establish regulations to promote safety, sanitation, and the conservation of natural and human resources wherever they are needed in the public interest, and to deal with pollution of the environment or interference with ecological balance.

Institute uniform intrastate standards for traffic arteries, for the flow of traffic, and for vehicles and operators of vehicles.

Establish regulations for dealing with labor disputes, and when customs, rules, strikes or other actions vitally affect the public interest or safety it may temporarily supersede the State or States and take such measures as are necessary, provided they are consistent with the laws.

Establish regulations for the manufacture, transportation, and sale of drugs; and notwithstanding the provisions under (1) of this section may with the consent of a two-thirds majority of the Senate federalize these functions.

Establish regulations for games of chance, betting, or any forms of gambling, including standards of licensing, taxation, and penalties for violations and infringements; and notwithstanding the provisions under (1) of this section may with the consent of a two-thirds majority of the Senate federalize these functions, but in such a case all moneys cleared above the costs of administration shall accrue to the States in which they are collected.

Section 10. *Exercise of Federal Powers by the States.*   Congress with the consent of the Senate, may assign to the States legislative and administrative control of certain Federal functions, not including any defined in this Constitution as belonging solely to Congress. These shall be granted for periods of twenty years at a time and shall be subject to duly stated guidelines and inspection; but may be rescinded in the case of any State by vote of two-thirds of each House.

Section 11. *Implied Powers.*
Congress shall have power to make all laws that shall be necessary and proper for carrying into execution the foregoing powers and all other powers vested in the Congress by this Constitution.

Section 12. *Qualifications of Congressmen.*   Congressmen shall be citizens of the United States, not less than twenty-five years of age, and though at the time of their election they need not be residents of their districts, they shall during their tenure be residents of such districts. All Congressmen and the members of the several State legislatures, and all executive and judicial officers both of the United States, and of the several States, shall be bound by oath or affirmation to support this Constitution; but no religious test shall ever be required as a qualification to any office or public trust under the United States or any State.

Section 13. *Congressmen-pro-Forma.*   To provide for continuity in leadership and experience, each party in the Congress that comprises not less than 20 percent of the elected membership may select as many as fifteen of its leaders not members of Congress to sit as Congressmen-pro-Forma, and in the case of a defeated party these shall include the defeated Presidential candidate; and they shall be certified by the Chief Justice and shall exercise all the privileges of membership, receive the same compensation, and sit and vote on committees, but may not vote on the floor except as provided elsewhere in this Constitution. In addition, former Presidents shall be Congressmen-pro-Forma for life except for such periods as they may hold other public offices of profit; but they may not at the same time hold office in both the Congress and the Senate.

Section 14. *Sessions and Rules.*   (1) Congress shall assemble at least once every year on a date it sets or when called into session by the President or the Chief Justice.

(2) A majority of the voting membership shall constitute a quorum to do business. A simple majority shall consist of a majority of those voting provided a quorum is present and voting, and shall be sufficient to do all business save where otherwise specified in this Constitution; but where a greater majority is specified, it shall be the stated majority of the membership entitled to vote. However, a smaller number than a quorum may adjourn from day to day, and may compel the attendance of absent members in such manner and under such penalties as Congress may prescribe.

(3) Congress may determine its rules of procedure save as stated herein, may punish its members for disorderly conduct and, with the concurrence of two-thirds, expel a member.

(4) Congress shall keep a journal of its proceedings and from time to time publish the same, excepting such parts as may in its judgment require secrecy; and, at the desire of one-fifth of those present, the yeas and nays of the members of Congress on any question shall be entered on the journal.

(5) Congressmen shall receive a compensation for their services to be ascertained by the concurrence of three-fifths of the full voting membership.

(6) In all cases except treason, felony, and breach of the peace, they shall be privileged from arrest during their attendance at the session of their House and in going to and returning from the same; and for any speech or debate in the House they shall not be questioned in any other place.

(7) During the time for which he was elected, no elected Congressman shall be appointed to any civil office under the United States (save within the Congress) which shall have been created or the emoluments of which shall have been increased by Congress during such time; and no person holding any office of profit under the United States or any State or local government shall be a member of Congress during his continuance in that office.

(8) There shall be stated times at which the President, Cabinet members, or their deputies may be questioned on the floor of Congress by members.

(9) Congress may require by law that Departmental policy orders be submitted to it, but such orders shall go into effect if no action is taken within thirty sessional

days by formal vote of Congress with the recording of the yeas and nays, or if Congress adjourns within thirty days without taking action.

Section 15. *Introduction of Bills, Motions, and Resolutions.* The President of the United States and the Senate may introduce bills, motions, and resolutions and, if they have not been acted on within six months, they must be brought to a final vote upon request of the introducer. Congress may not adjourn *sine die* until such a vote is taken, and all yeas and nays shall be entered on the public record. The President may espouse or refuse to espouse bills, motions, or resolutions introduced by other members or by the Senate (though he can not formally demand a vote on them within any certain time), but he may not prevent their introduction and consideration in committee; nor may he prevent the introduction and consideration by the Congress in open session or in committee of the whole of resolutions to censure or declare no-confidence in the President or Cabinet members and their deputies; however, Congress may not (save in case of the resignation of the President) force the resignation from office of a deputy or Cabinet member by vote of less than two-thirds of the members entitled to vote, and the vote must be taken in open session with the yeas and nays entered on the public record.

Section 16. *Congress Judges Its Own Members.* All members of Congress, whether elected, appointed, or pro forma, are subject (with the exceptions hereafter noted) to its jurisdiction and may be examined in cases of insanity or other disabilities, and their seats declared vacant, care being taken in each case to protect the rights of the member; and members may be impeached and tried by the body for crimes and misdemeanors, but may not be convicted without the concurrence of two-thirds of the membership; but judgment in cases of impeachment shall extend no further than removal from office and disqualification to hold and enjoy any office of honor, trust, or profit under the United States; but the party convicted shall nevertheless be liable and subject to indictment, trial, judgment, and punishment according to law.

Section 17. *Independent Agencies and Regulatory Commissions.* (1) To concentrate administrative responsibilities under the proper Cabinet officials, Congress shall not set up independent of them any regulative agencies or corporate authorities without the consent of the Senate, and those set up shall be subject to biennial review by Congress and the Senate and may be terminated by the consent of both. Nor shall such presently existing agencies be continued beyond five years at a time without the consent of the Senate. The members of all such agencies or commissions shall be under the rules of the Civil Service and shall hold office during good behavior or until they reach the statutory age of retirement for civil servants. But this shall not prohibit the Congress from setting up or from authorizing the States to set up corporate authorities to deal with public interests, provided always that they remain subject to proper executive and legislative authority and to the surveillance of the Senate of the United States.

(2) No bureau, agency, or corps in any Department shall be permitted to exercise the powers entrusted by law to another Department save on specific and temporary authorization by the President.

(3) No Executive agency or corporate authority shall exercise judicial functions, but Congress may create courts to deal with special categories of administrative problems and define their powers.

Section 18. *Hearings.* Congressional hearings may be closed to the public by the President or the concerned committee; nevertheless, the findings shall be published in the public record of the Congress within ten days of the conclusion of the hearings except in cases when the President certifies that such disclosures would be against the public interest.

ARTICLE II. THE PRESIDENT

Section 1. *The President.* (1) The President of the United States shall be the presiding officer of the Congress and chief of the executive arm of the Congress, and upon assuming office shall take an oath prescribed by Congress. He must have been a citizen of the United States for at least ten years or a citizen of a country that has become a part of the United States. He shall be charged with the executive duties of government, with the command of the armed forces, with making treaties and agreements with foreign nations, and all other duties assigned by Congress, and his actions shall be subject to the approval of Congress; but in no case shall approval of his actions, appointments, bills, motions, resolutions, and treaties require more than a majority vote of those present and voting, provided that those present constitute a quorum. Moreover, he shall from time to time address the Congress and the public on the state of the nation.

(2) Neither Congress nor the majority party caucus shall adopt a vote of censure or expression of no-confidence in the President with the intention of forcing his resignation without a week's notice, nor shall a President be forced to resign without the concurrence in a floor vote of a majority of the total membership of the Congress entitled to vote, with the yeas and nays duly entered on the public record.

(3) The President in office at the time of the adoption of this Constitution shall serve out his term, but in accordance with the provisions of this Constitution.

Section 2. *Presidential Succession.* (1) The President shall hold office during the five-year term of Congress and shall be eligible to succeed himself, until his death, disability, or resignation for private reasons; until he loses the support of the majority of the membership of Congress entitled to vote; or until removal after examination for mental instability or conviction for high crimes and misdemeanors. Congress may make the presentment for examination and may vote for impeachment of the President or a Cabinet Secretary, but in either case the examination or trial shall be before the Senate, and removal shall be only by a two-thirds majority. In the event of the President's removal, death, disability or resignation for private reasons, the Congress shall elect a successor, who shall serve during the remainder of the term with the same powers, privileges, and checks as a popularly elected President.

(2) The President may not ask for the dissolution of Congress save when he loses the support of his caucus or of the majority of Congress, but in such an event he shall have the right (unless enjoined by a three-fourths vote of the Congress) to require the Chief Justice to dissolve the Congress and issue writs calling for nomination of Congressional candidates, national Presidential nominating conventions, and elections, all to be held within not more than ninety days; and the President and Congress elected shall serve five years unless the term is sooner ended by Constitutional means.

Section 3. *Presidential Powers.* (1) If the President of the United States is not an elected member of Congress, he shall nevertheless hold ex officio membership, exercise all the functions Constitutionally provided, enjoy all the privileges of membership, including the right of voting on the floor, and shall be chairman of his party's official organization, of its Congressional caucus, and of its committees. When the President happens to be a regularly elected member of Congress or a Congressman-at-Large, his resignation from the Presidency shall not affect his standing as a member of Congress.

(2) The President may call Congress or the Senate into full session at any time. With the consent of Congress, he shall appoint from the elected membership of Congress, and may remove, a deputy to preside over Congress; he shall appoint, with the consent of Congress, from the elected membership or from Congressmen-at-Large, and may remove, Secretaries of Departments; and he may appoint, with the consent of Congress, and may remove, the deputies of the Secretaries of Departments, and if they are not members of Congress they shall become Congressmen-pro-Forma in addition to the regular fifteen as long as they hold office.

(3) At the beginning of each Congress and with the consent of the party caucus, he shall appoint the majority floor leaders of Congress and the majority members of all Congressional committees and sub-committees, and shall be chairman of those committees, but he may delegate the chairmanship to a deputy who acts as vice-chairman and who serves during his pleasure; but each Secretary of a Department shall be vice-chairman of the Congressional committee charged primarily with oversight of his functions.

(4) With the consent of the party caucus and notwithstanding the opposition of minority Congressmen, the President may strike out riders, rippers, clauses in pending bills, and items in appropriation bills, and provide that authorization of funds shall be tantamount to appropriation; and such decisions in caucus shall result in a unit vote being cast for all party members in any vote taken in committee or on the floor, though in the floor vote a member may ask to be noted as mute; but the unit rule shall not prevail in votes censuring President, Cabinet

Secretaries, or deputies, or calling for their resignation. On petition of one-third of the elected members of the caucus any vote in caucus shall be taken by secret ballot, with Congressmen-at-Large participating.

(5) With the consent of the Congress, the President shall appoint administrative officials and judges, except those judges and officials answerable to the Senate; and shall appoint and have the power to remove such other officials as Congress may by law provide; but in any appointment requiring Congressional approval (except that of Senators), if Congress does not act within thirty sessional days of the submission of a nomination, such nomination shall be considered as confirmed, and the adjournment of Congress *sine die* before the end of the thirty sessional days shall be considered as confirmation of the nomination.

(6) With the consent of Congress, the President shall appoint, and may remove, all other Federal officials not coming under Civil Service, save that Congress shall provide by law a right of appeal for those civil officials removed for cause, but not in a position to make executive policy and not under the Civil Service.

Section 4. *The Cabinet.*   Congress shall divide administrative functions among executive Departments, each of which shall be headed by an elected Congressman or a Congressman-at-Large appointed by the President and subject to removal by him. These Secretaries of Departments shall constitute the President's Cabinet and executive assistants and, together with their Congressional deputies and the majority floor leaders of Congress, shall constitute his policy counselors and Congressional aides. There shall be for each Department a Congressional committee, which shall have the right to draw on the facilities of the Department for purposes of studies, investigations, and drawing up legislation. The majority members shall serve as assistants to the Secretary and as trainees for possible future administrative functions. Minority members of the committees shall participate in policy discussions and the consideration of bills, and the leaders of the minority parties who are members of Cabinet committees, together with their floor leaders shall constitute Shadow Cabinets, whose function is to work with their party councils in formulating the policies of the opposition.

Section 5. *Executive Residence.*   Since the present Executive Mansion shall become the residence of the Chief Justice as Chief of State, Congress shall provide the President with offices near the Capitol, and with a suitable residence, together with such upkeep, staff, appurtenances, and salary as the dignity of the office requires.

ARTICLE III.   THE JUDICIARY

Section 1. *Federal Courts in General.*   The judicial power shall extend to all cases, in law and equity, arising under this Constitution, the laws of the United States, and treaties made or to be made under their authority; to all cases affecting ambassadors, other public ministers, and consuls; to all cases of admiralty and maritime jurisdiction; to controversies to which the United States shall be a party; to controversies between two or more States, between citizens of different States, between citizens of the same State claiming lands under grants of different States, and between a State and foreign nations.

Section 2. *Federal Cases in State Courts.*   The courts of the States are empowered to exercise original jurisdiction over cases arising within their borders under Federal laws, and Congress by general laws may instruct other States to turn over to them such fugitives, witnesses, and evidences as the circumstances may require; but appeals may be made to Federal Circuit Courts whose decisions shall be final unless the courts of the Senate consent to a hearing. However, a Federal Circuit Court or a Senate court may order that a case be instituted before a State court or lifted from a State court. Original jurisdiction of State courts over the enforcement of Federal laws shall not extend to cases properly belonging to courts authorized in Section 3, and in case of conflict over jurisdiction the decision shall rest with a Senate court of appeals.

Section 3. *Courts Set Up by Congress.*   Congress shall set up Circuit Courts to hear cases between citizens of different States bearing on matters in which there is a clash of jurisdiction between States and cases between citizens of the same State claiming lands under grants of different States; and to hear appeals on decisions on Federal laws made by State courts. It may also set up special administrative courts, such as Claims, Customs, Internal Revenue, Patents, Military Appeals, and Admiralty. Judges shall be appointed by the President with the consent of Congress and shall hold office during good behavior until the age of seventy. They shall receive a compensation that shall not be diminished during their continuance in office.

Section 4. *Functions of the Senate.*   The Senate shall be the highest court in the land, and the final judge on questions of Constitutional interpretation. It shall be devoted to preserving a rational balance among the parts of the Federal government and among Federal, State, and local authorities; to protecting the rights of the citizen; to observing and investigating the functioning of the laws and proposing such new laws and Constitutional amendments as it deems beneficial; and to acting in such other capacities as are specified in this Constitution.

Section 5. *Qualifications of Senators.*   (1) A Senator must be a citizen of the United States and not less than thirty-five years of age, and shall serve for life or until he reaches the age of seventy. There shall be two classes of Senators: Law Senators, learned in the law; and Senators-at-Large, not members of the bar, but chosen for their knowledge, integrity, and ability to deal with public affairs. A Law Senator appointed from a State need not be a resident at the time of appointment, but during his tenure shall be a legal resident of the State he represents.

(2) The Vice-President and Senators holding office under the Constitution of 1787 shall join with the Supreme Court to perform the functions of Law Senators

and Senators-at-Large according to their qualifications until the new States, as hereafter defined, are able to be represented. Supreme Court justices who have reached the age of seventy shall then retire, but those under that age may continue to serve as supernumerary Law Senators until seventy, but Senators under the Constitution of 1787 shall cease to hold office.

Section 6. *The Appointment of Senators.* (1) Each State shall be entitled to two Law Senators, but the remainder of the normal membership of fifty Law Senators shall be assigned to the States in proportion to population. After each census the proportion shall be altered if necessary to prevent an undue increase in membership. Those States entitled to additional Law Senators shall have them appointed, but the Law Senators from the States whose representation is decreased shall continue to serve until their retirement at the age of seventy, or until their resignation, death, or removal.

(2) Writs for the appointment of Senators shall be issued by the Chief Justice, and they shall be chosen as follows:

In the case of Law Senators, a committee of the Judicial Assembly of the State shall meet with a committee of the State Senate, the executive of the State, and the majority and minority leaders of the legislature and draw up a unified list consisting of three candidates for each vacancy, but of persons not necessarily residents of their state, though with outstanding legal or juristic qualifications. From this list the President shall present a name for Congressional approval; but in such cases the quorum shall be constituted by a majority of elected Congressmen, Congressmen-at-Large, and Congressmen-pro-Forma, meeting *in camera* and voting by secret ballot, and a majority of those present shall be necessary for approval. In case the nomination is not approved, the President shall select another name from the list to be voted on, and so on until a name is approved. However, in case the vacancy or vacancies are not filled, the slate shall be submitted to the Senate, and it shall meet *in camera* and vote for its choice or choices by secret ballot. In case both Houses reject the entire slate, the State must submit new nominations, but approval will then be by the Senate, meeting as before *in camera* and voting by secret ballot.

In the case of Senators-at-Large, the Chief Justice may receive nominations from any source, public or private, and such nominations shall be submitted to a Senate screening committee with a majority of Senators-at-Large (after the initial appointments) which shall select a unified list consisting of not fewer than three candidates for each vacancy. The candidates shall then be considered by Congress *in camera* under the same conditions as in the selection of Law Senators, and in case Congress fails to choose the Senate shall choose a member or members, meeting *in camera* and voting by secret ballot. The number of Senators-at-Large shall be fifty. Senators-at-Large shall at the outset take office as they are chosen.

Section 7. *Rules and Procedures.* (1) The presiding officer of the Senate shall be the Chief Justice, chosen as hereafter provided. The Senate's sessions shall be denominated by the calendar years, and it may not adjourn *sine die,* but may recess from day to day, and the Chief Justice or President may call it into full session.

(2) A majority shall constitute a quorum to do general business, with such exceptions as shall be made in this Constitution; but where a greater majority is specified, it shall be the stated majority of the membership entitled to vote. However, a smaller number than a quorum may adjourn from day to day, and may compel the attendance of absent members in such manner and under such penalties as the Senate may prescribe.

(3) The Senate may prescribe its rules of procedure save as stated herein, may punish its members for disorderly conduct and, with the concurrence of two-thirds, may expel a member.

(4) The Senate shall keep a journal of its proceedings and from time to time publish the same excepting such parts as in its judgment require secrecy; and, at the request of one-fifth of those present, the yeas and nays of the Senators shall be entered on the journal.

(5) Senators shall receive a compensation ascertained by a three-fifths vote of the membership.

(6) In all cases save treason, felony, and breach of the peace, they shall be privileged from arrest while on official business of the Senate, and in going to and coming from the same; and for any speech or debate in the Senate or any of its courts or commissions they shall not be questioned in any other place; nor shall any non-Senatorial official of the Senate be questioned in any other place on Senate business.

(7) No Senator may accept any other office of profit, public or private, and remain a member of the Senate; but this shall not bar him from accepting reasonable fees for lecturing, writing, or such related activities as the Senate may approve, or engaging in such temporary assignments and missions as the Senate may approve.

Section 8. *Judicial Powers of the Senate.*   (1) The Senate shall supervise Federal courts set up by Congress under such rules as are established by the Congress; shall establish procedures for the examination of Federal judges in cases of insanity or other disability, and may declare their benches vacant, care being taken in each case to protect the rights of the person being examined; and may impeach Federal judges for crimes and misdemeanors, but may not convict without the concurrence of two-thirds of the membership; but judgment in cases of impeachment shall not extend further than to removal from office and disqualification to hold and enjoy any office of honor, trust or profit under the United States; but the party convicted shall nevertheless be liable and subject to indictment, trial, judgment and punishment, according to law.

(2) The Senate shall erect from its Law members such courts of last resort as it deems necessary, and they shall have discretionary power as to whether to hear

cases on petitions for writs of *certiorari,* extraordinary writs, or ordinary appeals, and cases where a State is suing citizens or corporations of another State. All cases affecting ambassadors, other public ministers, and consuls, and those in which States are in conflict shall be heard before the proper court of the Senate.

(3) The Senate shall have the right to employ such permanent or temporary officials, not members, as it sees fit to aid in carrying out its Constitutional functions, and they shall be protected by uniform civil service rules laid down by the Senate.

(4) When an issue of Constitutional interpretation is accepted, after hearings before the proper court of the Senate and written opinions set forth by the justices, the matter shall be decided by the total membership of the Senate entitled to vote, but the matter may first be subjected to debate in the committee of the whole upon application of one-fourth of the Senate.

(5) The Senate shall set up a permanent court whose function will be to protect the rights of the citizen in cases of injustice or unreasonable delays, and it shall establish subsidiary panels of appointed judges, commissioners, or referees throughout the country to operate under such conditions and to exercise such powers as the Senate may determine; and the Senate shall provide for remedies in cases of injustice wherever that is possible, and may order the accused parties to be tried in the proper courts, whether Federal or State.

Section 9. *The Senate in Times of Crisis.*   In time of public disaster or peril from crime, subversion, invasion, rebellion, war, or other causes, the Senate, with regard to any or all forms of such disasters or perils, may suspend the writ of habeas corpus, authorize summary search and seizure or other extraordinary means of obtaining evidence (except physical or mental torture), or declare martial law, applicable to all or any part of the country; and if the Senate is not in full session the President or the Chief Justice may take action until the Senate returns in full session. But such action shall be confirmed only by concurrence of the majority of the membership of the Senate entitled to vote, and appeals in cases of abuse shall be available in accordance with law as provided by the Senate. In all votes taken under this section, the yeas and nays shall be entered on the public record of the Senate.

Section 10. *Power over Congressional and State Legislation.*   (1) By a majority vote of the membership entitled to vote, the Senate may suspend for six months any appointment or executive order of the President or a State's executive, or any legislation or article of legislation, or any appropriation adopted by the Congress or by a State's legislature, during which time it must be reconsidered by the authority involved, and if it is not reconfirmed at the end of that period it becomes null and void.

(2) By a majority vote of the total membership entitled to vote, the Senate may propose to the Congress or to a State new legislation or amendments to existing or pending legislation; if such proposals are made to the Congress by the Senate

three times in three successive years, and if each time the Congress fails to act, rejects them, or alters them to the dissatisfaction of a majority of the total voting membership of the Senate, the Senate by a two-thirds vote of the membership may dissolve the Congress, and the Chief Justice shall issue writs calling for national party conventions and new elections of Congressmen and of a President. In all votes taken under this section the yeas and nays shall be entered on the public record of the Senate.

(3) When a State legislature fails in three successive years to act satisfactorily upon a recommendation of the United States Senate for the reform of its judicial system or local government, the Senate, with the consent of two-thirds of Congress, may impose such reforms upon the State. Moreover, when under authority of Article I, Section 9, Congress lays down certain guidelines to the States for the exercise of their powers, the Senate may upon due investigation declare that the performance of the State is not satisfactory, and Congress may take over Federal administration of those powers and continue to exercise them as provided in the above-named article.

Section 11. *Studies and Investigations.*   (1) Upon its own volition or upon request of the President, the Congress, or any State, the Senate shall assign permanent or ad hoc committees or commissions to undertake studies and investigations, but the hearings and deliberations shall be closed. The Senate shall report on the results of such studies and investigations, making such recommendations as it deems advisable; but no report or recommendation shall be published until the completion of the study or investigation.

(2) All Senate commissioners, committees, and courts shall have the power to appoint attachés, to issue subpoenas and *subpoenas duces tecum,* and to summon or subpoena witnesses and expert advisers. The foregoing shall include any Congressmen or administrative officials and their papers not individually exempted by the President in a specific instance; but they may not be exempted in cases involving violations of ethical practices, or malfeasance or misfeasance in office. In cases of contempt such commissioners, committees, and courts shall have the power to remand the accused for trial according to such procedures and with such penalties as the Senate shall have provided; and in cases of misdemeanor or felony they shall have the power to order prosecution by the proper courts according to law. The Senate of the United States shall be empowered to recommend that State Senates take cognizance of the actions of administrative and legislative officials at State or local levels.

Section 12. *The Senate Judges Its Own Members and Officials.*   (1) All members of the Senate and its permanent or temporary officials are subject to its jurisdiction and may be examined in cases of insanity or other disabilities and their offices declared vacant, care being taken in each case to protect the rights of the individual.

(2) Senators may be impeached and tried by the body for crimes, misdemeanors, and breach of ethics, but may not be convicted without the concurrence of two-thirds of the membership. Judgment in cases of impeachment shall extend no further than provided for Federal judges in Section 8 of this article; but the party convicted shall nevertheless be liable and subject to indictment, trial, judgment, and punishment according to law.

(3) When a Senator or any official of the Senate not a member of the body is subjected to civil or criminal suit the Senate, to prevent harassment, may by a majority vote lift the case to the proper court of the Senate.

Section 13. *Budget and Property.* (1) The Senate shall set its own budget, which shall be accepted by Congress without change, and the Treasury shall pay all drafts made upon it by the Senate.

(2) The Senate shall be empowered to acquire, administer, police, and dispose of property, to exercise eminent domain, and to make all rules and regulations it deems useful respecting such property.

ARTICLE IV. THE CHIEF JUSTICE

Section 1. *Chief of State.* The Chief Justice shall be the Chief of State of the United States, and as such shall preside over the Senate, shall have ceremonial precedence, shall receive the credentials of ambassadors, shall authenticate all credentials, laws, treaties, and international agreements; shall issue all writs appointing commissions and calling for national conventions, and Congressional primaries and elections, and the appointment of Senators; and shall certify the results of such elections and appointments. He shall have the power to call either the Congress or the Senate into full session at any time.

Section 2. *Election of the Chief Justice.* The Senate shall elect the Chief Justice of the United States from among its members to serve a single term of five years or until he reaches the age of seventy if that be sooner, and he shall take an oath prescribed by the Senate. But the Chief Justice of the Supreme Court at the time of the adoption of this amendment shall become the presiding officer of the Senate for three years, and shall exercise all the rights and duties of the office. Former Chief Justices who may have resigned from the Senate shall be pro forma members of the Senate until the age of 70 except for such periods as they may hold other public or private offices of profit; but they shall have no vote, nor may they hold memberships at the same time in both the Senate and the Congress.

Section 3. *Powers of Appointment.* With the consent of the Senate, the Chief Justice shall appoint from the Law members of the Senate such courts of last resort as the Senate shall authorize, including one to deal with cases of constitutionality. The members of such courts shall hold office for ten years, or until they reach the age of seventy if that be sooner, and they shall be eligible for reappointment; but they may not be removed during their terms save in accordance with Article III, Sections 7 and 12. With the consent of the Senate, the Chief Justice shall appoint such permanent and ad hoc committees and their chairmen as the Senate shall provide for, and they shall have the powers heretofore specified. He shall appoint from the membership of the Senate with its consent, and shall have power to remove, such deputies as he deems necessary to aid him in his duties, and a deputy to preside over the Senate; and in case of the death, incapacity, resignation, or removal of the Chief Justice, the deputy presiding over the Senate shall perform the functions of Chief Justice until the Senate elects a successor; but in cases of examination or impeachment and trial of the Chief Justice the Senate shall elect a special presiding officer, and the presiding deputy shall have no part in the proceedings.

Section 4. *Executive Powers of the Chief Justice.* When there is a stalemate between President and Congress, or when Congress fails to elect a President to fill out a term, the Chief Justice with the consent of two-thirds of the Senate may dissolve the Congress and issue writs calling for national conventions and elections. In any interim between Presidents, the Chief Justice, with the aid of the permanent civil servants, shall administer public affairs until a President takes office.

Section 5. *Annual Report.* At least once a year the Chief Justice shall issue a report on the state of the nation addressed to the Congress and the people, giving the sense of the Senate on national problems and making recommendations for action.

Section 6. *Official Perquisites.* The Chief Justice shall have his official residence in the present Executive Mansion, and the Senate shall provide him with staff, appurtenances, upkeep, and salary compatible with the dignity of the office.

ARTICLE V. PARTIES, CONVENTIONS, AND ELECTIONS

Section 1. *Political Parties.* (1) The Senate shall pass uniform laws by which independent candidates and political parties shall be entitled to national or State recognition; but since democracy cannot operate without the agreement of the parties to formalized rules of political rivalry, no such candidate or group that advocates the forcible overthrow of any government in the United States shall be recognized as a candidate or a political party; and any applicant for elective office —Federal, State, or local—must swear to support this Constitution.

(2) The Senate shall pass uniform laws for the establishment of permanent national and State party councils. Their business shall be to foster national, State,

and Congressional district party organizations, and they shall meet at least once a year to coordinate State and national party attitudes and to formulate and interpret proposals for party policies and programs.

Section 2. *Districting.* Representatives in office at the time of the adoption of this amendment shall serve as Congressmen until the next regularly scheduled Presidential election, but for that election the existing Supreme Court shall apportion elective Congressional seats among the States; and thereafter the Senate shall apportion them after every census. Each State shall have at least one Congressman, and all Congressmen shall run on a general ticket; except that when there are more than seven the State shall be divided into districts without regard to the boundaries of local governmental units, each district entitled to a number of Congressmen as close to five as practicable, and the candidates of each party in the district shall run on a general district ticket. Such districts shall be as contiguous, compact, and proportionate in population as possible.

Section 3. *National Political Conventions and Campaigns.* (1) The Senate shall provide by law for the selection of Congressional candidates, for the selection of national Presidential nominating convention delegates, and for the governance of such conventions and national political campaigns, including the roles of communications media, and the raising and expenditure of money for the campaigns, and shall have power to enforce such laws. It may also appropriate funds for their financing from its budget according to a pre-set formula; but the finances for national party candidates shall be distributed through their Congressional central committee.

(2) The political parties shall hold national Presidential nominating conventions on call of the Chief Justice or whenever a Congress completes its term of five years, and in all such conventions the party's national and State councils, elected Congressmen, and chosen Congressional candidates shall be among the members; but the entire process, from issuance of the writs for election of Congressional candidates and delegates to the nominating conventions to the final Congressional elections, shall take no more than ninety days. The national Presidential nominating convention shall choose a Presidential candidate, and the choice of candidate and the party's statement of program shall be binding on all of the party's Congressional candidates and officials. If any candidate fails to support them but is elected, he may be excluded from the party's Congressional caucus and all party offices by the President, or in the case of a minority party by the defeated candidate for the Presidency.

Section 4. *Elections.* The Congress shall set the qualifications of voters in all elections—Federal, State, and local—but the Senate shall be the judge of congressional elections, and writs for such elections shall be issued, and final results certified, by the Chief Justice. In the Congressional elections each voter may cast as many votes as his district has Congressmen, but he may not cast more than one vote for an individual candidate. Independent candidates who are elected to Congress may be accepted as members of a party caucus but may not hold party or Congressional offices or committee assignments during the life of the Congress to which they were elected. The Presidential candidate whose party receives the plurality of Congressional seats shall be declared elected, and in case the two leading parties tie, the candidate of the one receiving the largest popular vote shall be declared elected. President and Congressmen shall assume office as soon as their election has been certified by the Chief Justice. Elections of Presidents and Congressmen shall not coincide in time with State elections, except that in case of the death, resignation, or removal of an elected Congressman, his successor may be elected at the most convenient time.

Section 5. *Congressmen-at-Large.* When a Presidential candidate is elected but carries less than a 55 percent majority of the Congressional seats he shall appoint (but may not remove) enough Congressmen-at-Large to give his party a 55 percent majority of the voting membership, and may appoint their successors in case of their death, resignation, or removal; and such appointees shall be certified by the Chief Justice and shall exercise all the rights, privileges, and duties of elected Congressmen, including the right to vote in committee and on the floor, and shall be counted in making up a quorum.

ARTICLE VI.   THE STATES

Section 1. *Composition of the United States.* (1) The United States shall be composed of States, Commonwealths, and possessions. The nature and powers of the States will be defined hereafter, and possessions shall be those areas considered too small or with inadequate resources or population to exercise more than limited autonomy.

(2) The Commonwealths shall be self-governing under terms laid down by Congress, but Congress shall retain control of foreign affairs, defense, and administration of the public domain. The people of the Commonwealths and possessions shall be citizens of the United States, protected by its Bill of Rights and Senate courts, and may elect pro forma members to Congress and the Senate as each body may determine. Alaska and Puerto Rico shall be eligible for commonwealth status, but the latter may opt at any time for complete independence.

Section 2. *Consolidation of States.* (1) Immediately upon the adoption of this Constitution the existing Congress shall set apart as new States the geographic areas outlined in the accompanying map and description, and where necessary provide for the survey and demarcation of the boundaries, with such minor alterations as are deemed advisable by Congress. However, in later years these boundaries may be altered or new States formed or old States consolidated from time to time by three-fourths vote of Congress with three-fourths of the

Senate consenting; and Congress shall provide by law procedures by which petitions may be filed requesting the erection of new States or the transfer of an area from one State to another.

(2) The purpose of the consolidation is to give greater viability and unity to the regions or conurbations contained therein and to enable them to shoulder more of the legislative and administrative functions hitherto exercised by the Federal government. It is recognized that no formula for consolidation can meet all the desirable criteria, but the consolidated States shall at the outset be as follows:

ALASKA: It shall vote on whether to become a Commonwealth or a part of Oregon.

ALLEGHENIA: Pennsylvania; Delaware; New Jersey south of a line drawn from the Delaware River to the Atlantic Ocean at 40° 18'; Maryland east of the northernmost point on the Potomac River at Hancock; the northern panhandle of West Virginia north of the protraction of the Mason-Dixon Line; Arlington, Fairfax, and Loudoun Counties, Virginia; and the District of Columbia, which shall lose its character as a Federal district and become an integral part of the State.

APPALACHIA: Kentucky and Tennessee except the parts west of the Tennessee River; North Carolina; the remaining portions of Maryland, Virginia, and West Virginia; and the part of Alabama north of the Tennessee River.

CALIFORNIA: From the Pacific Ocean eastward along the north line of San Luis Obispo County to the crest of the Coast Range; along the crest of the Coast Range to the Tehachapis and to Tehachapi Summit; thence west to the present eastern line of California; thence south along the present eastern boundary of California.

CHICAGO: From Lake Michigan follow the north line of Illinois to 89° west; thence south to the 41st parallel; thence east to 86° 45' west; thence north to Lake Michigan.

DESERET: Nevada; Utah; Arizona; the part of Wyoming in the Colorado River Basin; Colorado west of the Continental Divide, Sawatch, and Sangre de Cristo Mountains; New Mexico west of the Sangre de Cristo Mountains and Sacramento Mountains; El Paso and Hudspeth Counties, Texas; and the part of California not included in the new States of Sierra and California.

ERIE: Ohio; Indiana, except the part taken for Chicago; Michigan except the Upper Peninsula and the corner taken for Chicago.

HAWAII: Unchanged.

MISSISSIPPI: Minnesota, Wisconsin; Iowa; Illinois except the Chicago area; the present State of Missouri east of 94° and north of 37°; and the Upper Peninsula of Michigan.

MISSOURI: North Dakota; South Dakota; Nebraska; Kansas; the parts of Montana and Wyoming east of the Continental Divide; that part of Colorado east of the Divide and the Sawatch and Sangre de Cristo Mountains; and Missouri west of 94° and north of 37°.

NEW ENGLAND: Maine; New Hampshire; Vermont; Massachusetts; Rhode Island; Connecticut except Fairfield County; and the part of New York north of 42°.

NEW YORK: The remainder of the old State of New York; Fairfield County, Conn.; New Jersey north of 40° 18' North.

OREGON: Washington; Oregon; Idaho; Montana west of the Continental Divide and the strip of Wyoming west of the Continental Divide and west of the Colorado Basin.

SAVANNA: South Carolina; Georgia; Florida; Mississippi; Alabama except the part north of the Tennessee River; Louisiana except the part given to Texas; Arkansas east of 92°; Missouri east of 92° and south of 37°; and the parts of Kentucky and Tennessee west of the Tennessee River.

SIERRA: Follow 42° east from the Pacific to the eastern limit of the Sacramento River Basin; thence along the crest of the Sierra Nevada; along the crest of the Tehachapi Mountains to the Coast Range; thence northward to the north line of San Luis Obispo County and to the Pacific.

TEXAS: Texas as at present constituted except for El Paso and Hudspeth Counties; Oklahoma; New Mexico east of the Sangre de Cristo and Sacramento Mountains; Louisiana north of 31° and west of 92°; Arkansas west of 92°; and the portion of the present State of Missouri south of 37° and west of 92°.

Section 3. *State Constitutions.* (1) Within ten days of the adoption of this Constitution Alaska shall vote on whether to assume Commonwealth status or to become a part of Oregon. Immediately thereafter the judges of the highest courts of the old States shall meet in bodies, with the body in each new State composed of the judges legally resident therein. These bodies shall provide for the election within one month of Constitutional Conventions, and shall set the qualifications of candidates and the procedures for election to the Conventions. Each Convention shall be composed of not more than fifty members and shall meet within one month after election.

(2) The Constitutions shall follow as nearly as feasible the institutions set forth in this Constitution, with a unicameral legislature and an appointive Senate; and shall be submitted to the vote of the people. Each Constitution shall provide for greater consolidation of local governmental units and service districts, and more economical and simplified methods of administration. It shall also reform and enlarge the judiciary sufficiently to handle promptly cases arising under State and Federal laws, and shall create a Judicial Assembly; but judges shall not be popularly elected, and shall serve during good behavior or until the age of seventy.

(3) The State Senate shall lay out the districts entitled to representation in the State legislature, taking care that they shall be as contiguous, compact, and proportionate in population as possible, but do not coincide with the geographical units of local government.

(4) National party labels may be used by candidates in primaries and elections for the legislature or for State-wide offices, but not for county, municipal, or other local elections or run-offs; but in States where the municipality is coextensive with the State or in which in the judgment of the United States Senate one conurbation comprises the majority of the population, the United States Senate shall determine which offices may be sought under a party label.

(5) As soon as the new Constitution of a new State is adopted and the new legislature meets, the old States within its borders shall cease to exist.

Section 4. *Powers of the States.* (1) In addition to the foregoing, the States shall exercise the powers named in Article I, Section 9, but under the conditions therein stated.

(2) They shall also, with due regard to Article I, Section 9, have the powers to exercise eminent domain, to lay and collect taxes, and to borrow money; to regulate business and transportation carried on wholly within the State; and to regulate the standards of privately controlled schools and to maintain public systems of education. They shall exercise the powers necessary to maintain public order by the passage of necessary legislation concerning civil and criminal procedures, save as laid down by Congress, and the establishment of judicial systems; by raising and maintaining local and state police forces; by establishing prisons and places of detention and correction and conditions of parole and pardon; and they shall have the power to call out the militia in cases of invasion or public disasters and disorders.

Section 5. *Cooperation among the States.* In matters of common interest, two or more of the States may make arrangements with each other or set up boards or corporate authorities; but the Senate of the United States shall have the right to propose changes and, if the State authorities reject them, may order that they shall be submitted to the vote of the people of the States. Full faith and credit shall be given in each State to the public acts, records, and judicial proceedings of every other State, and the Congress may by general laws prescribe the manner in which such acts, records, and proceedings shall be proved, and the effect thereof. The citizens of each State shall be entitled to all the privileges and immunities of citizens in the several States. A person charged in any State with crime and found in another State, on demand of the executive authority of the State from which he fled shall be delivered up to be removed to the State having jurisdiction over the crime.

Section 6. *Powers Forbidden to the States.* (1) No State shall enter into any treaty, alliance, or confederation; pass any law impairing the obligation of contracts; or exercise any of the powers granted solely to Congress in Article I.

(2) No State shall lay a tax on Federal property or personnel save by consent of the Congress or the Senate as the case may be, but these Houses shall provide for such taxation or for contributions by general laws.

ARTICLE VII.   BILL OF RIGHTS

The following prohibitions are laid on the United States and all its States, Commonwealths, and possessions.

Section 1. *Freedom of Religion, Speech, the Press, and of Assembly and Petition.* They shall make no law respecting an establishment of religion or prohibiting the free exercise thereof; or abridging the freedom of speech or of the press; or the right of the people peaceably to assemble and to petition the government for redress of grievances.

Section 2. *Further Prohibitions.*   No bill of attainder or ex post facto law shall be passed, nor shall excessive bail be required, nor excessive fines imposed, nor cruel and unusual punishments inflicted; nor shall private property be taken for public use without just compensation.

Section 3. *Security.*   The right of the people to be secure in their persons, houses, papers, and effects against unreasonable searches and seizures shall not be violated, and no warrants shall issue, but upon probable cause, supported by oath or affirmation, and particularly describing the place to be searched and the persons or things to be seized. Exceptions may be made only in unusual cases involving treason, subversion, or serious crimes, but then only by courts and under conditions duly authorized by the Senate of the United States.

Section 4. *Rights of an Accused Person in Criminal Cases.*   (1) In all criminal prosecutions the accused shall enjoy the right to a speedy and public trial in the State and district where the crime is alleged to have been committed, which district shall have been previously ascertained by law, and to be informed of the nature and cause of the accusation; to be confronted with the witnesses against him; to have compulsory process for obtaining witnesses in his favor, and to have the assistance of counsel for his defense.

(2) No person shall be held to answer for a capital or otherwise infamous crime unless on a presentment or indictment according to law as laid down by the United States Congress and Senate, except in cases arising in the land or naval forces or in the militia when in actual service in time of war or public danger; nor shall any person be subject for the same offense to be twice put in jeopardy of life or limb; nor shall he be compelled in any criminal case to be a witness against himself, nor be deprived of life, liberty, or property without due process of law.

(3) Trials shall not be by jury, save that the accused may demand juries in cases of first degree murder or treason, and then three votes in four shall be sufficient to convict; but no death penalties shall be imposed. Grand juries may be formed to investigate matters of public importance, make recommendations, and present indictments.

(4) The death penalty shall be abolished in those cases where an accused is already serving a sentence of life imprisonment.

Section 5. *Slavery.* Neither slavery nor involuntary servitude, except as punishment for crime whereof the party shall have been duly convicted, shall exist in the United States or any place subject to its jurisdiction.

Section 6. *Definition, Privileges, and Immunities of Citizens.* All persons born or naturalized in the United States and subject to the jurisdiction thereof are citizens of the United States and of the State wherein they reside. No law shall be made or enforced which shall abridge the privileges or immunities of citizens of the United States except on conviction for crimes, nor which shall deprive any person within its jurisdiction of the equal protection of the laws; nor deprive any person of life, liberty, or property without due process of law; nor discriminate among them on account of sex, race, color, religion, or birth out of wedlock except in cases of inheritance as the courts may determine under law.

Section 7. *Right to Vote.* The right of citizens to vote shall not be denied or abridged by the United States or any State or locality on account of sex, race, color, or religion, or by reason of failure to pay any poll tax or other tax.

Section 8. *Party Rights to a Place on the Ballot.* In primaries and elections where party names may be placed on the ballot, no party certified as such by the United States Senate may be refused a place.

Section 9. *Titles of Nobility Prohibited.* No title of nobility shall be granted; nor shall any person holding any office of profit or trust under Federal or State governments accept, without the consent of the Congress, any present, emolument, office, or title of any kind whatever from any king, prince, or foreign State.

Section 10. *Regarding Rights Not Enumerated.* The enumeration in the Constitution of certain rights shall not be construed to deny or disparage other rights retained by the people.

ARTICLE VIII. METHODS OF AMENDMENT AND REVISION

Section 1. *Amendment.* Either the Congress or the Senate by two-thirds vote may propose an amendment to the States, in which case it shall be declared a part of this Constitution upon ratification by three-fourths of the legislatures, or when proposed to the national electorate it shall be declared a part of this Constitution upon approval of a majority of those voting. Any State may propose an amendment, and upon its approval by the legislatures of one-half of the States it shall be submitted to a vote of the national electorate.

Section 2. *Revision.* A convention for revision of the Constitution may be called by two-thirds of the Congress and two-thirds of the Senate, voting in the same calendar year, and upon consent of two-thirds of the States within the following five years as expressed by their legislatures and Senates; or the call may be initiated by any State and the convention held upon agreement of two-thirds of the States within a five-year period. Any revised Constitution may be adopted only by vote of the people.

ARTICLE IX. VOTING ON THIS CONSTITUTION

On its own volition or on petition of the legislatures of one-half of the present States, Congress shall set a date about one year in advance, at which time the people shall vote their choice: (1) to accept this Constitution; or (2) to call a Constitutional Convention to amend or revise the Constitution of 1787.

INDEX

3 5282 00314 7256